The Pearly Gates Phone Company

Chele Pedersen Smith

Hi Melody, Sept 16, 2021

I think you'll enjoy these spiritual shorts. Several take place in your home town. and you know some people mentioned.

For my family, on Earth and beyond.

*Contains bonus pages, "Beyond the Blessings."

Have you had your mini miracle today?

♡ Chele

My brother John Smith is "Jake." with an already alias name, he elected to have another alias.

Many thanks to contributors Jeanette, Joey, Linda, Stacie, Jenn V, Joe H, Janice, Dawn, Micki, and Rob and Lisa for recounting their remarkable experiences and allowing the privilege to share with the world.

Some names have been changed to protect the innocent.

Directory Assistance

Rainbow Sprinkles

Life's more interesting with God's touch.

I'm not a theology expert. I'm just an ordinary girl living a normal life. But when mini miracles began rocking my world, I knew I had to capture them in a jar.

When my dad called from Heaven, it was too remarkable not to share. It inspired the main story (Chapter 10) and title of this book. From there, I gathered other moments where God shone brightly, mostly on a smaller scale.

The first story, "Naivety Scene," has a message but also serves as a map of my childhood. It helps make sense of the changing scenery as the stories progress.

Some of the chapters might seem a little quirky, like making peace with a partially empty nest in "The Pancake Parable," finding creative ways for children to grieve by "Planting Crayons," and ditching the devil in

"Eviction Notice." I have a wacky way of looking at things so adding imagination and a dash of humor makes daily challenges easier to digest.

Thanks to friends, there's a serving of bigger miracles, too. Just wait til you see what God did in Kenya!

Maybe labeling a feature "The Funeral Follies" is a tad taboo. I don't mean any disrespect; it's truly devastating. But in my family, silliness seeps into somber ceremonies even when we're not trying. I always say life's a sitcom but the laugh track is real!

Comedies tend to have serious storylines so I'm not always amused. Other emotions run amok, but that's when faith steps in and rounds them up, and I hope these awe-inspiring stories do the same for you.

Amazing things are going on all around us. We just have to open our eyes, ears, and heart to see it. I bet you've experienced it too. I find nods of God just by looking in my backyard. A woodsy environment puts on quite a show, which proves God doesn't have to move mountains to let us know He's here. Sometimes the reminder we need is as small as an anthill.

|1| Naivety Scene

Maybe that's why Jesus said, "Let the children come unto me."

We boarded the plane in '73 not knowing fear. How I wish I had that freedom now. Not of travel or flight but being free of fright. We had no idea aircraft could crash, or any of the other dangers life dangled ahead. As youngsters, we didn't worry about a thing. Instead, we followed our mother on board and buckled up with glee.

"Are we up in the air?" I asked eagerly, when the winged capsule started to taxi.

"Not yet." I didn't notice Mom white-knuckling the arm rest or her choppy answer.

Ignorance *is* bliss. I was eight and Jake was five, and we were allowed to bring two toys. In one arm I cradled the stitched cloth body of a lifelike baby, passed down from Aunt Bobbie's childhood, dutifully named Barbara Ann. And naturally, I chose Chrissy.

Purchasing my dream doll with birthday bucks the year before, I couldn't part with the eighteen-inch figure tucked beside me. I loved her groovy orange dress and matching boots. But most of all, I was mesmerized by the miles of cinnamon mane swinging past her behind. If I wanted to bob her hair, voila! I could wind a knob on her back and reel it in. I still have her today, though she didn't fare very well during my teenage makeover years.

If I recall, Jake chose his Sesame Street Ernie puppet and maybe a car. Each armed with our favorite playthings, we were ready to embark on a life altering adventure.

The whole thing was a miracle really, because just weeks before we were trudging through Connecticut snow to the corner store when Mom broke the news.

"We're moving to Hawaii!"

"Yay!" my brother and I cheered, our Island knowledge limited to Gilligan and The Brady Bunch.

Jumping up and down like we won a

prize, a crushing reality hit as soon as my boots skimmed the sidewalk.

"Oh no, we'll be leaving the family!"

Grandmom and Grandpop were drop-by regulars, sometimes with a dozen Dunkins in tow, and always with an interesting trinket. Our two aunts helped Mom out often, and our little cousins were constant sidekicks. But the worst goodbye at the airport was Dad.

He and Mom divorced the year before, although we kids didn't know the difference. My free spirit father was trying to make it big with his rock bands, so he wasn't always around.

That same year we shared a special bond over piano lessons. Jake tagged along and they waited in the hall while I plinked the ivories. Besides spending time with Dad, our favorite part of the hour was Dairy Queen dipped cones.

Other memories involve mustache-tickled kisses, playgrounds and his guitar strumming carnival tunes as we coasted down slides. Going to actual fairs for fairy floss and fried dough, and his narration of Harry Nilsson's story "The Point" at bedtime in different voices. Sometimes he would put on puppet shows at the foot of the bed. Even though we didn't see him as much as we hoped, funny how my mind chooses to remember the times we did.

Now it seemed magical leaving a harsh January behind, leis replacing scarves as we traipsed across the tarmac into Oahu's warm, fragrant night. It was as if we stepped foot into a far-fetched Disney dream.

On the runway's reverse was redheaded Jimmy, our soon-to-be-stepfather. He and Mom were on and off again high school sweethearts. He joined the Navy right after, and Mom met hippie-musician/artist Andy during hangouts with her sisters at Savin Rock Amusement Park in West Haven.

Mom and Jimmy reunited in the honeymoon haven of the fiftieth state, tied the knot quietly while we were in school, and thus began the cultural experiences of two sheltered kids as we transferred coast to coast.

Two weeks left of wearing flip flops to school and learning Japanese art, a midnight jet launched us to California, the ascent feeling like a straight-up rocket!

In Cali, a baby brother was born along with the love of Mexican and Filipino food, the San Diego Zoo, and Major League Baseball stadiums, a passion that's followed me through many states and teams. And we really did get to see Disneyland—twice!

Sixth grade diploma in hand, we celebrated America's Bicentennial cross-country in a compact car. Talk about family togetherness! And what a great geography lesson. For instance, I learned Arizona doesn't help cool things down when you roll down the windows. Thank goodness for motels pools.

Cutting through Texas, overnighting in Missouri, we headed north for a relatives' reunion before trickling south to our new duty station in Orlando's Navy housing. Which was good timing because that's where the Freedom Train chugged in at the end of its tour. And what luck to be out biking! Twenty-six cars filled with 500 Americana artifacts and all I remember is Dorothy's dress.

When Jimmy retired from the military, the folks bought a house from scratch in nearby Union Park, and we thought our moving days were over. But when school was out, we were at it again.

Five years of Florida in the rearview mirror, we rattled around in the back of a covered pick-up truck en route to the Land of Lincoln. Stopping to cool off in the Chattanooga caverns of Ruby Falls has always been a highlight of that trip. An underground waterfall is a gorgeous wonder!

Along for the ride with hardly a protest, each excursion of our childhood was enriched with experiences I never could have imagined. Why couldn't I treat every aspect of life with the same blind faith? It was easier as a child when adults were in charge; I figured they knew what they were doing. But when that adult is me, there are too many choices, too many possible wrong turns. Too many people to please. Fear whispers defeat in my ear. I'm bogged down by cognitive baggage.

But Jesus wants to lighten the load. He wants us to rely on Him, not please everyone else. "Come follow me. I will make you fishers of men." Matthew 4:19.

He wants us to revive our youthful innocence and childlike trust. "Therefore, whoever humbles himself like this little child is the greatest in the kingdom of Heaven." Matthew 18:4.

So I'm trying to be *less mindful* these days, keeping Jesus in the foreground, letting His voice override wavering doubts. I'm learning to drop my net full of worries, which should be pretty easy for a klutz like me. But I'm a work in progress.

|2| Point of Sail

Do you remember your first prayer? Or the macramé craze of the 70s?

Rough twine knotted nicely as the plant hanger took shape on the back of my door. My temper tugged the strands together with a little more force than necessary.

"Stay here in case the phone rings," I mimicked.

Why was I the one always left behind? Just because I was the oldest, it wasn't fair. As a twelve-year-old, I still enjoyed family outings. But it wasn't like I had a choice. I couldn't exactly switch places with Joey, my three-year-old brother. And my middle sib was obligated to attend since it was his scouting event. I knew Mom and Jimmy weren't being mean. Just practical. We needed a bigger car. We all crammed into the tiny Volkswagen Rabbit for the occasional

Mystery Fun House trip or back-to-school shopping. But for ordinary errands, if it wasn't necessary to drag three kids anywhere, I was the designated answering machine.

I was looking forward to the Webelos Regatta. Jake diligently sanded and painted his project, and it was shaping up great. Now I would miss the results because I was stuck home waiting for a phone that never rang.

Still miffed, I hopped off my desk chair to grab some beads. Spying my turntable, I spun a Donny Osmond album. Maybe some swooning would help my mood. Thinking about the Osmonds' tight-knit family gave me an idea. I could cheer my brother on from home!

A recent dream popped into my head, the vision still crisp: a magnificent cross rising from the horizon, glowing against the backdrop of the sun. When I woke, its majestic power brought tears to my eyes.

We'd just started going to Sunday school in the McCoy Naval Annex's re-purposed barracks in '78 with my new friends Debbie and Maggie. Our teacher, Mrs. Cooke, was teaching us about prayer and Matthew 7:

Ask, and it shall be given you; seek, and ye shall find;

Knock, and it shall be open to you.

Hmm, I had never tried it. Well, not formally anyway. I sent up hopes and wishes as I drifted off to sleep. Did those count?

Now was the time to test it for real.

I felt dumb asking God to rig a Boy Scout boat race, but the tantalizing power of prayer nagged me as I finished my craft. Was it even fair? What would it hurt? It was better than moping.

"Please God, let Jake win the race. Thank you!" I kept it simple and went back to fringing the end of the planter, not really holding Him accountable for the outcome.

When I heard the rattle of the kitchen door, I greeted my family in the living room. "Did you win?" I dutifully asked.

When my brother held up a first place

medal, looking proud but embarrassed, I couldn't believe it. And when Mom and Jimmy took turns gushing, "All the other boats had drag, but Jake's took off with zest," I was floored. But God was showing me, a newbie in training, that I *could* believe—in Him. Even with a silly sailboat, He was the Captain in command.

|3| Jesus '81

Are you ready for an old-fashioned revival?

Scorching in the Orlando heat, Jesus was alive and well.

He wasn't hard to find amid tents of workshops and marionettes as our youth group setup camp for the weekend. We sacked out in metal pop-ups, which were surprisingly comfy— and roomy too. Capable of squeezing in a bunch of us for endless rounds of Uno or a fierce game of Pit. The card trading frenzy often resulted in a riot of, "Barley," "Oats," "Wheat," "Rye" as we scrambled to be the first to collect a one-of-a-kind hand.

After a muggy day of sessions, beads of sweat clung to me. Not the most flattering accessory for an awkward adolescent. Cranking open cans of tuna, my contributing chore for the evening supper, I knew the humidity would drop soon and the best part of the day was yet to come.

I loved sunset best. We relaxed in folding

chairs by the main arena, bathed by the cool breeze under the stars. The evening was pure joy as contemporary Christian music floated from the stage. Sometimes they'd throw in a comedy act, and we'd always be blessed with inspiring thoughts to carry us through the night.

At sixteen, I tried maneuvering to sit next to my crush—another reason to like downtime. But I didn't want to appear obvious, so it didn't usually pan out.

Geoff was our church organist, a prodigy, preppy and cute, and an all-around nice kid. When I discovered he was left-handed, my fascination grew even more, and I practiced writing southpaw just in case I ever needed to. But alas, the affection was unrequited, so I had no choice but to settle for friendship, which wasn't easy for my restless heart.

After breakfast, we'd gather around the main stage for morning worship, soaking up prayer and words of wisdom before flocking our separate ways to the exhibits.

"Trying is a sin," the speaker's voice boomed. "When you claim to be something, you either are or you aren't," he continued. "If you are trying to quit lying, but you slip up, you're still a liar, aren't you? If you're trying to quit stealing, but have sticky fingers, you're a thief. If you're *trying* to be a Christian, then you aren't really one, are you? You aren't true to Christ in your heart."

I'm paraphrasing since it's been so long but the gist of what he said always stuck, and at the time I found it worrisome. As if we teens needed something else to confuse us. Wasn't trying a good thing? If we don't try, we fail, some sayings go. Now if we try, we are sinners?

Our leader, Mrs. Eva, broke it down for us and as I decipher it now as an adult, I think the man was telling the dots of people that we need to give it 100 percent. We're either in or we're out. Kind of what Yoda was teaching the Jedi.

For some reason with the glare of sun

and prickles of heat, these sermons felt more like thorns.

That is, until the next morning when a different speaker chose the theme of loving your neighbor as yourself or something like that. "Turn to the person behind you and greet them with a kiss," he instructed.

This was different. What happened to a handshake? I wasn't too keen about laying one on a stranger, but before I could scope out the prospect, the person in front spun around, his crooked smile aiming my way. Geoff! Oh, gosh, this was really happening. He leaned forward and brushed his lips quickly across mine.

My first kiss, and with the organist of my dreams! I was stunned. But it happened so fast, I wish I savored it or at least, reciprocated. Either way, thank you, Lord! A reward for my patience.

I floated through the final day. But Geoff's lips weren't the only impression left on me that weekend. The experience was so uplifting, my soul really felt revived! For the next week or two, my emotions overflowed onto paper. I composed the song, "I Found Love." Well, it was only lyrics, so basically it was just a poem.

Contrary to the smooch, the hymn wasn't about *him*, but Him. A strong urge nudged me to share this in church, but how if I couldn't write music? I really should've paid attention to those piano lessons. Tapping my pen against my notebook and wishing Dad lived closer, I scanned my room for ideas, thinking. Then my eyes fell on my tabletop organ. Ah, I knew just the person!

Funny how infatuation sets up the perfect scheme. But I doubted he'd want to collaborate. What if he thought I was back for more, trying to make something happen, something besides the song?

I broached the subject after church. As he collected the sheet music, I gathered my nerve. I hurried over before he joined his folks in the fellowship hall, trying to squelch my squirming stomach.

"Hi, Geoff. Guess what?"

"Hey. What's up?"

"I wrote a song." I pulled the paper from my Bible and handed it to him. "I was inspired at the festival." In the slice of a second, I could feel my cheeks turn hot. "About God," I rushed, in case the title made him run for the hills.

"That's great. Do you want to play it?" He stepped back to make room.

"Well, no, it doesn't have music. I was hoping you could help with that?" Suddenly the whole idea sounded lame and see-through. I felt like an idiot. Planning a quick getaway in my head, I thought I misheard his response.

"Sure!"

"Really? Oh, thanks! Um, see you tonight at group." I hurried off on cloud nine before I made things worse.

Since he had the piano, we met at his house the following Saturday. In his room, in fact. I was bubbling nervously and tried my best to maintain a pseudo-professionalism as I contributed my lyrics, which I am sad to say I lost over time. The words escape me and I wish I had them now. I wonder if they were any good.

For a while, Geoff tried creating an original tune, but in the end, we molded the words to the melody of Gene MacLellan's "Snow Bird," made popular by singer Anne Murray.

When we crafted the song to near perfection, we ran it by Pastor Gill. With his approval, we churned out copies to sing at the next evening service. What a glorious, yet humbling experience— Geoff's talent on the keyboards, the congregation singing the praise God streamed through me. A triangular team effort.

And hey, having an excuse to spend time with the boy I liked didn't hurt either.

|4| Soar like an Eagle

Chums since Cub Scouts, then Webelos and Boy Scouts eleven to thirteen, Joey's troop was a tight pack. Besides baseball with most of the same kids, scouting in the mid 80s was one of the best times of his life in Waukegan, Illinois. Several buddies were also neighbors.

Mom was co-den mother with Mrs. Harvey until Joey and the boys earned their Arrow of Light and moved up in rank. Jimmy and other dads pitched in, but the main leader was Mr. Groat, a man in his eighties.

Passionate about scouting, his own kids had long outgrown the uniform, but Mr. Groat could still keep up with the best of them. Blue and Gold banquets and other awards, raffles, adventures, camping, pancake breakfasts, (my favorite stop before church!) and the most important of all, community projects.

He encouraged his troop to strive for Eagle Scout. It was the highest achievement a scout could earn. He wanted his boys to take pride in themselves. His goal was contagious. It had many of the fathers and sons eager for Eagle, too.

The big Tri-State two-week outing was upon them, so the troop packed up and headed to Muskegon, Michigan. They most likely set up camp at Owasippe, the oldest Boy Scout site in the United States.

One morning halfway through the event, Mr. Groat collapsed in the bathroom cabin while chatting with Jimmy. Scrambling to shuffle the scout master to the van, Jim, Mr. Tarbox (another dad), Joey and his friend Roofer zipped off to Muskegon Hospital. But sadly, Mr. Groat died along the way, right in front of the boys.

The rest of the day was a fluster of shock, consoling the scouts, and making phone calls. Camping was cut short, but before leaving, the troop put together a little memorial service.

During the tribute, although sad and shaken, the guys were comforted knowing Mr. Groat died doing what he loved. Then circling overhead, Joey spotted an eagle, the highest honor, indeed.

|5| Sudden Impact

Our attitude affects others. Sometimes it boomerangs
right back!

The May air crackled. Even the elements
keeping us alive knew something was about to
combust. Yeah, me! Maybe it was hormones
causing the crankiness. Or the most likely
source— the New London DMV.

The Illinois plates were about to expire,
and I was doing my darndest to switch over to
Connecticut. Instead, I was the one flipping
out. I arrived elated, having just paid off my
'84 Chevette, but these party poopers were
destroying my happy dance.

"Miss, I see James is listed on your title.
Is he here with you today?"

"No, he's in Florida. He co-signed my
loan, but I made payments and own the car."

"That explains why his name is on the
title," the monotone said. "He'll need to sign
this form to remove it. We can't proceed until

he does." The man handed me the paperwork. "Next!"

Arggh. It's like they secretly delight in finding a glitch. The red tape was ridiculous. I was twenty-three and married two years to Barry, a Navy fella, but now I needed my stepdad?

After seven years in the Midwest, Mom, Jimmy and Joey had just moved back to Orlando. It wouldn't have been so bad in this day and age, but 1988 didn't have internet or fax technology, which meant shipping the form Overnight Express! I left there in a huff, swinging the door hard out of frustration. I didn't care that it slammed the brick wall but was relieved it didn't break.

My bad mood carried me home. How annoying to find a humongous delivery truck blocking my parking space! I was quite bitchy to the men.

To my chagrin, I had to go out on another errand, but it gave me the chance to apologize.

For the next few days, I'd have to lie low with expired plates. No problem, I was a law-abiding citizen.

It would've gone off without a hitch if I hadn't locked the keys in the car during a Girl Scout outing! Just for fun, I co-led a troop, and we had just returned from a bus excursion to New York City and the Statue of Liberty. Helpful parents wanted to call the police, putting me in a pickle, but what choice did I have? We only had one car so it wasn't like my guy could come to my rescue.

While the officer collected info, I strategically blocked my license plate and he got to work sliding the doohickey in the door. I would've been home free if he didn't have to check my registration for ownership. Thank goodness he was understanding!

Finally, Jimmy's signed document arrived and everything was legal again.

One drizzly morning a week later, I was a street away from my desk job at Boyer Realty Maintenance when BANG!

I was covered in glass, screaming like a horror movie queen. *What was going on?* Confused, I stared at my windshield, but it remained intact.

A passerby checked on me through the driver's side. "Are you okay?"

When he spoke, I realized the window was gone. Because of the slick conditions, a car had rammed into mine almost head on.

An ambulance arrived. As the medics loaded me on a stretcher, I mumbled my work number to onlookers, hoping someone would call me out. Then they whisked me off to Lawrence & Memorial Hospital down the road.

I was fine, just glistening in glass with a few minor cuts, prompting a tetanus shot. As a precaution, they flushed my eyes meticulously, which was nauseating.

From a pay phone, I caught Barry up to speed, letting him know he needed a ride home, then called my coworker to pick me up. I hoped she knew why I was late.

"Yes," she said. "A man with broken English called, saying, 'Girl in accident, went to hospital.' Are you okay?"

"Yes, just scratched and shaken."

God bless that man!

I considered finishing the workday, but Joy drove me home instead, which was a smart idea because I realized then how wiped I felt.

Over the next few days, I was in agony. My arm, heavily infused with toxoids, felt like lead and my neck was killing me. I followed up at the base and they dished out what they did best—800 milligrams of Motrin.

It relieved the strain, but I wish it helped emotionally. The traumatic slam of shattered glass haunted me as I mourned the loss of my first car, our only mode of transportation.

Barry consoled me, always the great comforter in my rare breakdown moments, reminding me how the car saved my life.

If not for a buddy, we wouldn't have been able to get a rental. We had the rider on our insurance and we were going to pay cash, but if you're under twenty-five without a credit card, you're out of luck. Fortunately, Rob had plastic.

We swung by the auto yard to assess the damage. The Chevy was declared "totaled" so I was surprised it didn't look that bad. Still, I was devastated. It was the end of "Todd." It didn't feel right not to repair him. Well, we had a good run, I guess.

I opened the door to claim the remains. I was shocked to see the driver's side mirror sitting on the passenger seat, surrounded by shards. So that's what broke the window! But how did that clunky thing whiz by and not crack my noggin?

Collecting the items in my glove box, I shoved the usual paperwork and girly auto repair manual into the tote bag when something caught my eye.

"Hey, look at this."

I pointed to a thick volume sprawled on the floor of the backseat. Picking it up, I carefully shook glass from the pages.

My daily devotionals! I read one every morning when I parked at Boyer. Something told me this was the real source of safety. My guardian angel was a stow-away all along.

|6| The Turn-Around

Transferring with hubby's orders to Newport News, Virginia in the summer of '89 was exciting. Still kid-free, at least for another year, it was fun exploring new territory. We were fortunate to be only an hour from my inlaws in Richmond, but I was sad leaving my relatives and good-natured Dr. Wollschlager in Groton.

At twenty-four, I was on top of the world, freshly graduated from Huntington Institute and psyched to be his bonafide dental assistant in my new career. He was a patient, enthusiastic mentor hosting our class through externships.

Now I was starting over. When two interviews shed light on lesser pay than Connecticut, I was bummed. One practice even suggested temping through an agency.

So I checked it out. But the interviews they sent me on were ones I could easily find in the paper.

I started to second-guess my line of work, thinking I should've skipped straight through to hygiene school. Still, I dutifully kept the next appointment, even though the office was looking for a part-timer. Bummed, I relayed my dilemma, and received a surprising perk.

"You have the skills to make a decent wage," the woman told me. "You should be able to find full-time work, and you don't need the temp agency taking a cut. Plus our lower cost of living should make a difference."

Whew. I didn't mean to sound greedy but besides pitching in with our finances, I had student loans to repay. I didn't get the job, but maybe better; I left with a confidence boost.

Maybe I was ready to pursue Dr. Wollschlager's suggestion. He sent me off with well-wishes and the name and number of a colleague here in town. I had called his office early on, but he wasn't hiring. It wouldn't hurt to remind him with my resume.

With renewed spirit, I set out to find his practice. Here in my new town, the roads were a bit different than I was used to. If you wanted anything on the left side of the street, there was a special lane between the long barriers that divided the main stretch of Jefferson Avenue. Since I'm not the most finessed driver, it took practice to get the timing right, which was especially tricky on the lookout for address numbers.

When the professional arts building came into view, I finagled to the left and crossed over into the parking lot.

Oops. I misjudged and ended up next door. I considered maneuvering back onto the road and swinging in. *Better yet, I'll just park and walk over.* When I looked up, I realized I was standing in front of another dental office. *Hmm, I wonder if they're hiring.*

Job advice from Jimmy fluttered into my head... or was it God? *Drop in anyway.*

So I ventured inside. Mustering courage, I introduced myself to the receptionist.

"Do you have any openings by chance?"

"Oh, wait right here." Turns out, she was the manager and the dentist's wife! Shirley took my resume and went to fetch her husband.

I got the job on the spot. Yes, Robert Diggs, D.D.S. needed a second assistant, but they never advertised. They put the Lord in charge of Human Resources instead.

|7| S.O.S

October of '98, the submarine had just pulled out of port in the Mediterranean when the blood test came back positive. There could be an extra chromosome. Stateside in Groton, Connecticut, research consoled me logically. I knew accurate results were tricky to pinpoint at the sixteen-week pregnancy mark but in the back of my mind, I was a wreck. And now Barry couldn't be contacted for two weeks.

Already at risk for preterm labor from my first pregnancy, I axed amniocentesis and scheduled an intensive ultrasound early the next week. But I didn't want to go alone. Bringing eight-year-old Ian this time around seemed inappropriate. My mom lived in Florida and due to other obligations, my dad, an hour away, wouldn't be able to make it either.

He attempted to lift my spirit though, reminding me how loving and remarkable people with Down syndrome could be.

"Remember Corky!" he cheered, referring to the amazing Chris Burke in the early 90s' show, "Life Goes On."

Of course, he was right. The baby would be wonderful no matter what, but I couldn't stop the tears. Hormones and his odd consolation snowballed into feeling downright slighted. Even with advanced notice, my usually sensitive pop didn't want to rearrange a ride to work for my grown sister. I knew it was silly, but probably the only time I felt sibling rivalry.

I inhaled deeply, trying to stay calm. False positives were common, and the good Lord wouldn't give me something I couldn't handle. Still, if only I could talk to my hubby...

"Jesus, could you tap out a special Morse code to him?"

That night I dreamed the doorbell rang, and there was my sailor, ditty bag and all, standing on the doorstep. I woke up feeling reassured and thanked God for the sign.

Later that day, the phone rang. It was my Sea Dog! The boat suddenly needed a repair and had to dock near civilization. Hearing his voice was all I needed. Whatever happened, now we were on the same page.

A few days later, time for another brave breath...

The technician measured thumbs and examined other criteria...

And exhale. The sonogram and our daughter were just fine.

|8| Planting Crayons

Because children need a way to grieve too.

We hadn't lost a family member in twenty years. So the shock shook us to the core when Aunt Bobbie lost her battle with colon cancer that summer in the new millennium.

Only fifty-eight, she was a fierce fighter to the end of her three-year war. There was a slight remission but even during nauseous rounds of chemo, she hardly missed work, showing up at Mountainside, booking weddings and parties at the venue in Wallingford. She looked fab as Mother of the Bride in 1999, and glowed brighter still as a grandma shortly after.

The loss was a blow to her children, Stacie and Jeff, barely thirty, but probably hardest on her mother at eighty-one. But as usual, Gram remained stoic, just as I imagine she did when she became a widow in 1980.

When we lost Grandpop, none of the kids

were allowed to be involved. Even when he was in the hospital, my brothers and I made cards but stayed in Florida while Mom flew to Connecticut to rally with the grownups.

They were protecting us under an umbrella, a hush-hush where children are neither seen nor heard during death rituals. But is it healthy? It doesn't give us closure like it does for adults. Our folks were shielding us from sorrow with good intentions, but maybe they also didn't have the strength to dig through the avalanche of questions we were sure to ask.

Being a young church-goer gave me swagger, so I prayed for Gramps after his heart attack. No sweat. I knew a guy— *The Guy*—so naturally he'd pull through. But God took him anyway.

Boy, was I mad! What a let down from the breezy sail of prayer He showed me a few years earlier. In protest, I refused communion the following Sunday. There, that would show'em!

My grandfather's void plucked me from my blissfully ignorant teen world, a place where I never gave an iota about such dark ideas. Now I walked around in a dazed stupor. It was like being hit with a 4x4. Suddenly, I questioned everything.

Were we all born stamped with an expiration date?

Why were we here at all?

Did we pass through a pecking order, starting out as amoebas, bugs, animals, and working our way up to humans?

These thoughts zipped by like meteorites as I sat in my friend's driveway, scrutinizing the stars.

"How far do you think Saturn is?" Roberto asked.

"I don't know," I answered, staring off as we marveled at the Universe. I wondered where Heaven was if space was so infinite.

I wanted to be a nurse ever since age four and I was in the middle of first year Latin, something Grandpop beamed about. Now I wasn't so sure. Hospitals meant death.

With Mom away, Jimmy tried to cheer us up by taking us bowling with friends, our favorite pastime. Joking with our buddies normalized things, and the physical activity helped with our aggressions. But we still mourned our pranking patriarch.

He loved to goof around with his seven grandkids, serving us pot roast strings when he carved up Sunday dinner. He'd divert our attention by pointing to the ceiling then nab something off our plate. Or he'd pretend he had a dog, snapping his fingers with a "Come here, boy."

Our World War II Army chef never quite got the hang of cutting portions at home when he whipped up his Pennsylvania Dutch delights: sticky buns, scrapple, coleslaw, and our picnic staple—pickled (red beet) eggs.

Gram had a hand in her share of specialties too, like stove top chicken pot pie with yummy "slippy dough" squares, my favorite part. And sometimes she'd wrap apples in the scraps for baked dumpling treats. We were incredibly lucky Grandmom and Grandpop spent a Floridian Christmas with us just the month before. He had just turned sixty.

For a week or so, Grandpop appeared in my dreams. Nothing extraordinary though, nothing spiritual. No secret messages from beyond, at least none that I deciphered. Just glimpses walking down city streets, trying to catch up, shouting his name. I'd wake up in tears, missing him, but in the big scheme of things, it didn't really seem like he died. He was just away on a long trip. Not having gone to a ceremony, we didn't have a tangible way to signal the sendoff.

In true fashion, I didn't stay mad long. Eventually, faith brought back peace and our neighbor and church chauffeur, Mrs. Eva, answered my questions the best she could. The biggest lesson being God has his own plans, and we don't always get what we want. At least not on our timetable.

Fast forward to summer in the next century, and here we were at the wake, staring into our aunt's casket. We had small kids of our own, yet I was the only one who brought mine along. I got some odd looks from other guests.

My nine-year-old was close to his great-aunt. They had fun times, and he needed finality, a way to say goodbye. I wasn't about to let the confusion we went through baffle him.

"It just looks like she's sleeping," Ian remarked, relieved.

His sister Maizie was only a year old, so she probably didn't know what was happening, unless maybe subconsciously.

Funeral rituals were new to our folks too. They fumbled with the formality and details.

When Mom lost her father, they honored his wishes.

He always said, "No memorial service. Don't need any hypocrites. Just toss my ashes in the Atlantic."

Grandpop loved to fish, and that's where he wanted to spend eternity. So sprinkles it was. Turns out it didn't give the adults any more closure than us kids. No definite place to visit, set flowers, or say hello. Although we did wave to the ocean on a few occasions, once even sending carnations out to sea.

Realizing services were for the living, Bobbie's sisters threw a wake with a funeral the following day and a cremation soon after. But it wasn't until November thàt they chose a place of rest and had a stone engraved.

As we gathered among the autumn leaves, Ian was sad to lose his coloring buddy and felt compelled to push crayons into the earth.

"So she doesn't get bored in Heaven," he explained.

We choked back tears. How does a child know just how to get us?

But my son had the right idea. It's helped him connect with the cycle of life as we lost more relatives along the way.

Children need a way to grieve, honoring the special bond they have with a loved one. It doesn't have to be crayons, but don't rainbows look a little more vibrant lately?

|9| Radiance

She lies beautiful in death

swathed by angels

murmuring their song

til nothing's left.

She glows

An aura kisses her lips

and she evaporates, pristine.

Spinning her soul

into cotton candy wisps.

She glows,

her halo

radiant

~Chele

3/4/17

I've acquired a muse. I notice it happens most when I have a heavy heart. In the past year she's followed me thrice now. Whole poems practically form as I fall into bed. It's an unexpected gift, the opposite of writer's block. Especially since I rarely write poetry.

I think of muses as angels God sends down to inspire our talent. Greek mythology defines them as *inspiration*, which literally means *breathing* ideas into our souls.

As much as I appreciate this free offering, it also means climbing out of a warm bed to write it all down lest I forget by morning. Otherwise, I lie there for hours, burning these perfect words into my brain, keeping me from precious sleep.

This particular arrangement was a bit unsettling as I crawled under the covers. "She lies beautiful in death" are hardly comforting words as someone shuts their eyes. *I hope it's not me...*

After getting up and scribbling it down, I

trusted Jesus would wake me so I could continue with this book idea.

The poem bugged me for days. I loved the airy wistfulness, but I couldn't figure out what it meant. Then it finally hit me. It was my last living image of Aunt Bobbie.

The morning of her passing, we gathered around her hospital bed holding her hand, kissing her forehead, telling her how much we loved her, how much she would be missed.

Even half-out of it, feverishly babbling, she was quite beautiful.

In her delirium, she managed to quip, "I'm not dead yet!" leaving us a parting gift of laughter.

The lovely contrasting glow was a private observation I had tucked in my pocket. Overshadowed by our family's grief, I didn't think much about it until Aunt Linda remarked the very same thing a day or two later!

It was a comforting tidbit I forgot all about until this poem emerged from nowhere.

Why now, seventeen years later? Why the last edge of February, and not June, the anniversary of her passing? But ah, Aunt Bobbie's birthday was just a calendar turn away. It was another gift— just in time to share with family who miss her so.

|10| The Pearly Gates Phone Company

The call came from my dad's apartment that weekday afternoon in 2002. It wouldn't have been remarkable except for the fact he died of liver cancer the month before and his wife was reluctant to step foot in their apartment ever since.

Even more astonishing, I wouldn't have been home at that hour if three-year-old Maizie hadn't been sent home sick from daycare. So I answered, expecting to compliment my stepmom for her bravery. She must finally be sorting through his things! I had been asking her to let me know so I could help too.

"Laur! Good for you—" I cheered but stopped. It was an automated credit card recording, rambling mid-way through its spiel.

I double-checked the caller ID. It most

definitely showed *Smith*, *West Haven*, and dad's digits. I hung up confused and then speed-dialed the number only to get a busy signal. *Weird*. I pressed the key anyway to get a call back when the line was no longer busy. A few minutes later, a series of odd rings jingled. What I heard next sent me into emotional vertigo.

"*Hi, this is Andy...*"

Sobs suffocated my lungs, and I couldn't breathe. My father's deep, smooth voice sounded like a radio announcer. Closing my eyes, I took in the essence of the man with the gifted pipes. He was a talented painter and musician, who sang in Doo-Wop/Rock bands around the New Haven area in the 60s and 70s. Someday I would play his records again but not yet.

There were times I wanted to dial his answering machine just to hear his voice but didn't think I could handle it and here it was—calling me!

I've felt guilty not being at Yale sooner.

He was admitted twice, and the kids and I *did* visit the first time. My six-foot-one father looked frail swimming in the sheets, and his iconic voice was so hoarse from cancer spreading to his lungs. I was grateful for that lengthy phone convo we had the week before, even if it was raspy.

I wanted to pop in for coffee but he wasn't up for it. What do you do then, respect their wishes or barge in anyway? Funny how devious guilt can be, convincing us that we can never do enough.

The hospital released him shortly after his first stay and I thought we had more time. But two weeks later he was back. We lived an hour away, and I was working full time at a new job, juggling bills and Ian's sports schedule as a single mom with an impending divorce. In the scurry of the evening routine, I often forgot to check the internal voicemail, so we didn't get to him until practically the last minute.

The kids and I raced to Yale to say

goodbye. Well, it was as fast as we could get there considering distance, Friday traffic and locating my son, out on a hike with his nature class. My sister was pacing nervously in the hallway, waiting for us as we careened off the elevator with a speeding stroller.

"The priest is coming to read last rites," Charmel informed in tears as we hurried into the room.

Jake was already at his bedside holding one hand while Laura's fingers interlaced his L.O.V.E knuckles. Dad was unconscious. It was too late; there would be no more encores.

He looked young for sixty-three with his natural jet black hair, gray only flecking his mustache and beard. I kissed his forehead, using his nickname for me. "Dad, your Sunshine is here." But did he really know? It was such a haunting question.

And now, miraculously, here he was on the other end of the line. My knees were weak, and I had to lean on the counter, sure they would buckle at any moment. When the message ended, I shakily paged my stepmom. She responded immediately, and when I explained the phenomenon, we both had chills. As it turned out, she had *not* been back to the apartment and in fact, was in the process of having everything shut off.

I'd be lying if I said I didn't feel freaked when we hung up. But I was more at peace than I've ever been. Relief was replacing grief. I was still a good daughter; he knew how much I loved him and I did plenty of things for him, with him. And that was enough. I sat down in awe, feeling blessed beyond measure. Dad just said hello from Heaven! Thank you, Jesus, for patching him through!

⌘

The call wasn't the only strange thing that happened. Two other signs blew my mind. About an hour after dad's death, I ran inside a grocery store in West Haven to grab juice boxes and snacks for the kids before hanging with family at Dad's sister Charlotte's nearby. Later that month, when my bank statement arrived, the transaction read: Shop Rite, West *Heaven*. More than a coincidence or just a wacky typo?

Shortly after, my good buddy Rob happened to send a message at the end of a long trucking gig.

"Hi Sunshine, I made it home okay."

Odd, he didn't usually give that kind of shout out and he certainly never called me by a pet name before.

Dad always worried about me and insisted I let him know I got home after a visit. Now he was doing the same. There were no doubts about my father's whereabouts. Message received loud and clear

|11| Jesus for Hire

It had been a long time since I made a fast friend, especially one I could say outlandish things to and not worry about sounding like a Jesus freak.

I can pose wacky theories on Jeanette, who's editing this book, and she gets me. We met in 1983 at the Navy's electronic school at Great Lakes Naval Base in Illinois. The sea of sailors was like working in an eye-candy store for two girls under twenty. We had our pick of the crop, and we were picky. (We also had amicable *Journey* vs. *Police* wars.)

One date led to marriage in '86, which is how I ended up in the Nutmeg State for most of those sixteen years, albeit the one move to Virginia. How does the saying go? Join the Navy and see the worl, err...rotten Groton! It's not a bad thing. I was happy to live close to my relatives, especially Dad after all those years away.

Barry brought Rob home from sub school in '88 and he instantly became family. Still is. (We got a lot of mileage that summer from a six dollar hibachi grill— a quest Barry sent me on to get over my fear after the car accident.) Even far away, he's still someone I can say crazy things to and it doesn't faze him one bit.

You know it's organic when it just clicks. It happened again in 2003 when Michelle, an Army wife, wound up as my desk mate in the "Submarine Capital of the World."

I taught her office protocol while the dentists were away on vacation, but there was more gabbing than training going on. Before we knew it, we were trading stories about our pasts and our faith.

Newly divorced, a friend was just what I needed. But we didn't want the dental assistant in the back room ratting us out, so we made sure to get some work done.

When we were back in business, it

became apparent two receptionists with the same name would sound confusing, so Dr. Judy asked if one of us had a nickname. And presto chango, that's how Micki came to be. All these years later, I still call her that.

We'd occasionally have coffee on our days off or run errands. I liked that her minivan played contemporary Christian music and her Pampered Chef parties lured my interest back into recipes and food again.

Micki's oldest boy, MJ, was ROTC and joined the Army after graduation, serving a term in Iraq. I admired her faith of steel pulling her through until he was safely on America's turf again.

Over time, neither one of us worked at the dental office, but we'd still get together for coffee now and then. Her other son, Josh, was in high school, same as Ian, and with my daughter in full-day kindergarten, we had some free time to catch up.

One gorgeous day in May of 2005, we went for a walk. Micki was in the process of adopting Noah, eighteen months. She had been fostering him since he was seven weeks old. But she still had hurdles ahead to make it permanent. She was worried about her preliminary court day on the 11th.

She related her qualms as we strolled with the baby.

"I'm so nervous. We aren't allowed to have a lawyer with us."

Suddenly, I stopped in my tracks. "Jesus will be your attorney!"

We stood there prickled in goosebumps.

This incredible revelation could only come from the Good Lord above.

"Picture Jesus sitting next to you. Everything will be fine!" I said.

We chuckled a bit at the image. Would the Lord wear a suit and tie, carrying a briefcase, or would He be draped in His white robe? It would certainly be appropriate for a judge's chamber!

Whatever His attire, His presence was definitely "amicus curiae!"* The proceedings were cake, and a few weeks later on June 6th, they were cutting into one as Noah became a legal part of the family! He's been an entertaining blessing ever since.

Four years later, they adopted two young brothers from Haiti, Samuel and Joseph. Micki's boys (and two grandkids) keep her busy, and she wouldn't want it any other way.

*amicus curiae: legalese, Latin for "friend of the court." A third party entity who is interested but not part of the case and submits formal briefings of advice. (Merriam Webster Dictionary)

|12| The Pancake Parable

Got the empty-nest jitters? "Old Trusty" can help fill
the void.

It was the greatest kitchen scandal to go down
in culinary history. At least in my book and
according to my son, who was keeping track.
It even surpassed the great graduation cake
demolition of 2008. That was a fiasco I
thought I'd never live down!

Even as an experienced baker, I wasn't
immune to cooking calamities. This time I
was innocently transferring Congo Bars to a
Tupperware container when I was startled by
a sharp crack.

Just one piece left, and it had been
particularly defiant. Wedging the ancient
Ecko spatula between the corner of the glass
pan and the last chunky square had done the
trick. I was victorious, but at what cost? I
gazed in shock at the brown plastic fragments

scattered in the dish.

I didn't know whether to laugh or cry. Old Trusty had been in our family for over twenty years. I held up the handle to show my teen daughter and whimpered, "I guess I should've greased the pan better!"

Maizie gasped in horror. "Maybe we added too many chips."

That couldn't be. It was our first attempt but my cousin's recipe called for a variety of chocolate, peanut butter, and butterscotch morsels. A *Congo line* of flavor. Well, whatever the reason, the spatula was ruined now.

Half-joking, I immediately sent a photo of its disarray to Ian, by now a working college student. He didn't keep in touch as often as I hoped, but I thought he would want to see what happened to his old friend. He was the one who named the utensil back in high school because it was the best in our dwindling collection. It was reliable; sturdy yet flexible, making it easy to turn over grilled cheese sandwiches, eggs, or lift cookies from a baking sheet. But not stubborn dessert bars, I mused.

I took a deep breath, trying to be mature about the loss, and placed the flipper gently in the waste basket. My heart panged. I couldn't stand it, so I fished him out again. How could I let go of the apron strings, if I couldn't part ways with a cooking gadget? I chided myself for being silly and tossed him back in the trash. Being sentimental was complicated.

My little guy flipped pancakes with it when he was three. He even made some for Mr. Bear, the kindergarten companion who took turns visiting each child for the night. Years later, his little sister learned the fine art of flapjacks too.

A notification *ding* snapped me back to the present. I don't know which surprised me more; Ian's spontaneous reply or his strong reaction as emails flew back and forth that night.

"Treason!" my son declared in mock

outrage. "I demand that you institute an embargo on Congo Bars forever. We don't need a corrupt baked good."

Did I mention he was a business major? Maybe he should go into politics instead.

All kidding aside, he confessed to missing Old Trusty because none of the spatulas at his dad's place lived up to its standards. Finding the casualty both funny and sad, he urged me to keep the old thingamajig.

"Don't throw out O.T! Retire him instead. There will never be one like him again. You wouldn't throw out your Derek Jeter cut-out just because his career is over."

He had me there. I noticed Ian had abbreviated the beloved gizmo's name with initials. How appropriate; the poor guy surely put in the overtime.

Glad I wasn't alone in this tragicomedy, it was a relief that we had one more thing to connect us besides our enthusiastic love for baseball and comparing notes on *American*

Idol. Who knew it would be something in my kitchen caddy?

It was a tough year adjusting to a partly empty nest. When I married a scientist in 2005, I thought I anchored down a civilian life, never having to deal with relocation again. But I didn't count on layoffs. When we transferred the next state over for Bob's new job in 2012, my son remained to finish his degree. On top of that, I had to quit my pharmacy job, a place I had thrived for six years. Never mind my nomadic childhood, this was the hardest move ever.

Do you know that persistent prickling you get when you forget something important? Multiply that by a thousand.

Even though he was an adult and we were only two hours away, it still felt wrong leaving Ian behind. He moved out the weekend before we did and I nearly lost it over hot dog buns in the store the next day. I didn't care for this new dinner math for three.

On closing day, Bob handled the

paperwork while May and I strategically stuffed my car with suitcases, leftover groceries and cleaning supplies, clearing just enough room for Buster, our fourteen-year-old golden retriever. My jam-packed mind focused on having to meet the moving van by a certain time, so I was caught off-guard by a tsunami of tears as Ian's exit shot past on the highway. Maybe they should make those suction-cupped window signs to warn other drivers: *Emotional Mom On Board.*

The first few days I unpacked crying jags with opened boxes as we set up our new home. Would I ever get used to this?

Feeling blessed to have him under the same roof for twenty-two years was only a small consolation. Logically children grow up. They aren't ours to keep forever, merely loaned to us from God. All I could do was pray each night—for safety and smart decisions. Only when I pictured him covered in the bubble wrap of Jesus could I relax and drift off to sleep.

On my way to bed, I plucked the pieces of the spatula out of the trash— again. That's when I noticed something. Isn't our Lord like Old Trusty too? *Reliable,* always there when we need Him. *Sturdy,* giving us strength when we call upon Him. *Flexible*, not so rigid that He can't forgive us.

The bittersweet mishap opened my eyes. I could rely on Jesus to calm the sea of separation anxiety by having faith in Him, putting my children in His hands.

And I hadn't lost the bond with my firstborn just because he no longer lived with me. We were adapting to the home stretch of childhood milestones. Was there a section in the baby book for this?

My son's new-fangled independence occasionally pulls me into a colossal vortex of worry. When it does, I pray harder and stay busy! Remembering the exhilarating freedom young adulthood brings helps too.

It's not an easy fix, but as time passes, it does get better. I don't always know where he is, and he probably isn't eating his vegetables, but I'll cherish whatever moments I get, even if it means getting sappy over something as trivial as a pancake turner.

Two years later, Derek Jeter *did* retire, but he'll always have a "stand-up" career in this house. Plus he's keeping our newer golden, Penny, in line. She tipped him over once as a pup and has been leery of the looming cardboard ever since! Just saying his last name does the trick.

|13| Eviction Notice

Do you kick negativity to the curb? Have you ever taken it to the next level?

Something oppressing was in the air. Something darker than the dreary January skies. The torment started as soon as the idea of going back to school entered my mind. It was exciting, but the anxiety went beyond the normal set of nerves. Finally, I could get that elusive dental hygiene degree. When I tried before in previous years and states, the schools weren't exactly commuter-friendly. Now, in our new town, I lived only twenty minutes away!

I've graduated from technical schools for quick health care careers, but I've always dreamed of having a degree to feel complete. So, as an avid learner and classroom nerd, why was I dragging my feet?

Maybe it was speaking a goal out loud. Yikes. Now I really had to go through with it.

My husband was supportive. Maybe too much so. It was comforting Bob had my back so encouragingly, helping, more like propelling me through the hoops of registration. Slow your roll, mister!

Why was I so nervous? I should be hitting the "Add Class" button like a boss, but instead, I was trembling. The trepidation of committing my free time to homework and studying added to the mix. What if I wanted to scrapbook or work on my novel instead? After a long hiatus, I had just returned to fiction writing. Also, what if I no longer had it in me to get A's at forty-nine? Worse yet, what if my husband expected me to? Ah, now we were scratching the surface. And then there it was: math. I would eventually need *three* classes and be forced to face my phobia!

All these wavering doubts reached a crescendo. The week seemed full of calamities and anguish. A favorite glass broke. I felt outraged over the simplest thing. I screamed alone in the car to let off steam. This torturous feeling was so unusual I wondered if I was meant to go to school at all.

I had just one obstacle left. Checking off the immunization form. An hour before my appointment, I rifled through my blue college folder for good measure. I've kept everything I needed tucked inside all along, but suddenly, a shot record was missing! I needed proof of that vaccine series. I ran to my room and frantically searched another folder. I poured the contents of a manila envelope on my bed. Childhood report cards, baptism certificate, sixth-grade citizenship award, but not the verification I needed.

This was so strange, I was convinced a leprechaun was running amok.

Defeated and aggravated, I rescheduled with my doctor, and then out of desperation, did something I've never done before.

"Get Out of my House, Satan! Leave NOW!"

I never heard my voice bark an order with such authority. Penny ran for her crate.

Molecules of peace diffused through the air. I immediately felt better than I had all week. With renewed vigor, I resumed my search. Thumbing through the same blue folder, then sorting through the contents of the orange packet again: *Abracadabra,* there it was! I couldn't believe my eyes. How it got mixed in with old report cards, I'll never know, but one thing's for sure—giving an unwanted guest the boot was the kick in the pants I needed!

⸰⸰⸰

Going back to school was the best thing I've done in long time. If you're on the fence about it or any dream, go for it! My first class, Foundations of Algebra, was just right. I went in with clammy hands but relaxed as soon as I read the syllabus. Backtracking into digestible pieces, I consider my professor a math angel. Not only did his patience restore my confidence, his name disappeared from the faculty list soon after. Did he earn his wings?

|14| Riding Shotgun

Has something unexplainable ever saved you?

Midnight muddled their surroundings. Were they still on the highway?

My friend Jeanette was fresh out of high school and her sister Tabra just a preteen when their dad's post-Air Force job with Orkin in Orlando sent him to Tallahassee. Since it was temporary, Hal hung out in a pop-up camper.

Every weekend, his wife, Betty, corralled the girls and her own mother for the ambitious four-hour road trip each way.

One night, leaving the state capital particularly late, Nette's mom soldiered on behind the wheel while her passengers slept.

Jeanette remembers being in that dreamy realm of half-slumber where the glare of headlights distorted ordinary objects. Were her eyes playing tricks or were they heading straight for a pile of bricks?

"Betty!"

Suddenly her mother jolted awake and managed to wedge the car between a sign and a building.

Whew...

Now fully alert, the family sat stunned, praising the Lord.

"It's a good thing you called Mom's name," Nette marveled, thankful for her grandmother's deep voice.

"No," Grandma confessed. "I didn't say a word. I was asleep too."

|15| Hummingbird Hangout

Flying into the open garage, probably attracted to Bob's old red Mustang, a hummingbird found itself trapped.

It hovered near the ceiling for over an hour, and the more it flitted, the more we fretted. Offering peach juice in a shallow cup, we hoped we could pass it off as nectar, but nope, didn't even register on its radar. We pulled a flower stalk out of a bush, as suggested by the internet but that failed too, not having the right kind of blossom. The bird finally rested overhead on the garage door mechanism.

"Just fly down a little lower!" I coaxed. We waited with bated breath, but the creature didn't take my advice. Then my daughter suggested I say a prayer—this from my doubting teenager! Duh, why didn't I think of that?

"Jesus, please, send the bird down to us

so we can guide it out!"

Within a minute, the bird swooped toward us, slid down a snowsuit hanging on a peg, landing right where Maizie could scoop it up. With delicate care, she set him free! We stood there stunned, relieved, but mostly in awe. My daughter held a hummingbird, a rare privilege in itself, but it was God's instant message that spoke volumes!

|16| God Loves a ~~Cheerful~~ ^{Fearful} Giver?

Do you give freely or is something holding you
back?

"I'm pregnant and hungry, can you spare
some change?"

The disheveled girl popped out of
nowhere as traffic echoed off the cement walls
in downtown Worcester. And here I was,
stuck between an outreached hand and the
arm of a security gate.

"Sure," I said, even though I wasn't. I
plucked the two singles I had set out ahead of
time.

With my view partially blocked by the
machine, I couldn't spot any obvious signs of
conception in her layered clothing, but of
course, it was completely possible she wasn't
far along yet.

Still, I couldn't shake the subtle
shiftiness of the situation. Clearly, Jesus was
ashamed of me for being a skeptic, and I

didn't blame Him one bit. He was a pro. Me? A skittish city wimp. I wanted to help; I just didn't want to be played. Or worse.

Saving time setting out bills and quarters in my console cup was a wasted effort. The pay station only took plastic. The concrete maze was quiet, no rush. So I relaxed, card poised, skimming the directions. Alone before noon, I felt reasonably safe but mostly lucky winning Madonna tickets from the nearby radio station. Now I was edgy.

I was glad when the girl and her thanks ricocheted away.

Relieved, I refocused my efforts on the technology ahead, leaning over to swipe my card.

"Do you have a quarter?" Her re-emergence was jolting. I handed over four.

"Thanks so much," she expressed, slipping away as swiftly as she appeared. Transaction finally complete, I was free to roll, an act of kindness paid forward. But then I caught a glimpse of my gas cap—open!

Well, that spoiled the spirit. Strange, it wasn't ajar when I got in. Paranoia pushed the panic button while intuition whispered a warning. Was there a second person tampering with my vehicle while she distracted me? That old trick...

The fuel indicator remained full, so nothing siphoned. Once back on rural roads, I pulled over to peek, and all was well. Maybe it was just a failed attempt, or somehow in an unusually contorted feat, I managed to step on the pull-up lever, set flush under the steering column to the left and high above the emergency brake. Hmm, yeah, it was a real head scratcher.

The tainted experience left a poisonous taste, losing my appeal for goodwill and radio contests, fearing panhandlers and parking garages.

Months later, still subtly shaken, I snubbed a solicitor outside a cinema. Did I just flunk out of Good Samaritan 101? Feeling terrible, I immediately vowed to help the next person in need.

"I won't deny you three times, Lord!"

Still, wavering doubts wormed their way in while wiring a wad to a friend in need, a recovering addict. This led to a charitable chat with my aunt who often gave to the New Haven homeless. That's when it occurred to me. If we're to give, it should be free, out of love, not fear, no strings or second thoughts.

Suddenly my frightening encounter didn't seem so odd. Maybe I just had three dollars ready that I didn't need.

|17| Say What?

Do you hear God calling? What is He telling you to do?

Ears in tune for the Lord? Now there's an area that's always been a struggle. I'm terribly indecisive, not wanting to make the wrong choice for fear of regrets or ill consequences. I wasn't always that way, but after a segment of bad judgment, I noticed I've become hyper-vigilant ever since. So how and when do we know we're getting instructions from above?

Is it in church, as we sit obediently in His reverence? During bedtime prayers? My intentions are good, but it's hard to concentrate when my mind wanders. And listing people to pray for only churns the mill for hours.

Do we hear him in solitude, in quiet moments on a mountaintop? We're definitely getting closer on this one, but we don't need the motto or high altitude hairdos of the eighties. It says in Exodus 14:14, "The LORD will fight for you; you need only to be still," and in Psalm 46:10, God says, "Be still, and know that I am God; I will be exalted among the nations, I will be exalted in the earth."

Nice! So all we have to do is be quiet and listen. Easy, right? Not so much, especially in a smart phone world.

Along these lines without knowing it, I tried going on a picnic with Jesus once. I was eighteen. I packed lunch, a favorite book, and my writing tablet, which was actually paper back then. My destination wasn't far, only down the street by the high school. I was almost out the door and would've gotten away with it if Mom's nap hadn't ended just then. Knowing how protective she was against my going anywhere solo, I thought endorsing God as my bodyguard would help my case. Nope. She thought the whole idea was idiotic instead.

Well, another way I think Jesus speaks is by revving up gut feelings. He gave us this built-in radar so we'd know when something doesn't feel right. And we should heed its warning. And then there are times God is calling us *out* of our comfort zones to serve Him or change our situations for the better. We need to follow our instincts there too.

I'm good at listening when it's obvious, but sometimes when the voice is vague, and I'm torn between choices, I like to "toss the laundry up in the air." Now, I don't do this literally because I'm not fond of putting away clothes and don't want more chores for myself, but you could make a game of it if you wish. I picture a heap of clothes free-falling and by the time they all land, my answer kicks in loud and clear. How we really feel is already there, buried inside. We just have to brush away the junk clouding our verdict.

The most important way I think we hear Him is when sudden ideas or impulsive kindness strikes out-of-the-blue.

A few years ago it happened at an Illinois Olive Garden. Jeanette, her sister Tabra and their folks, the husbands, and Tab's young adult children were celebrating Mother's Day.

Nette's nephew Adam heard a loud clicking in his ear.

"Grandpa, did you just snap your fingers near my head?" When Hal said, "No," Adam was sure the Lord was trying to get his attention. Perhaps someone near was in crisis?

Their server stopped by to check on them. "Is there anything else I can get for you?"

They assured her they were all set.

"But maybe there is something *you* need?" Adam fished. Such bravery from a young person!

As it turned out, there was. She was fretting an upcoming eviction. So right on the spot, they held a tableside prayer circle. Later they left a big tip. Jeanette only wishes they knew what transpired next but she's sure an answered prayer came through one way or another.

In eleventh grade, my ears were more conditioned because besides church, I also attended Visions a few days a week. Voluntarily held at 7 am at Colonial High in Orlando, it's a wonder the busses got us there so early! It was a small, joyful fellowship with songs, scripture, and testimony—a very uplifting way to start the morning. Mrs. Hinson, my favorite Lit teacher, went too.

One day I noticed new student Minh-thawh fumbling with all her books. I caught up with her as we left class. She didn't speak much English, but somehow we conveyed understanding.

"Do you have a locker?" I asked, probably pointing to a row.

She shook her head no.

"Here, you can share mine." I signaled for her to follow. The metal cubbies were long and wide, plenty of room for both our books. I tore a piece of paper from a notebook and scribbled down the combo. She thanked me with smiles and nods.

For the rest of junior year, we were locker buddies. I moved over the summer, so hopefully, she got her own when school began.

I realize we could've just gone to the office in the first place, but it didn't occur to me at the time. These are the impulsive ideas I know must come from God.

Just like stories I've heard where strangers suddenly decide to volunteer as donors and match! In some cases, upon removal of said organs, cancer is discovered and cured, saving two lives at once— the ultimate good deed.

|18| The Funeral Follies

A funny thing happened on the way to the funeral...

Act I: Comedy of Errors
Keenan Funeral Home
West Haven 2002

My sister was notoriously late and Dad's funeral was no exception. As immediate family, we had the honor of sitting in the respectable front row so it was obvious she was missing.

Only a few minutes til "go time" and our stepmother was rightfully frantic. We had already said our farewells as Dad lay peacefully decked out in his Bronx Bombers best. Ian tucked a mutually favorite Matchbox car into the coffin, and we promised Papa we'd always save a seat for him at Yankee

Stadium.

Now his wife turned to me. "Give her a call and see where she is?"

Being new to a cell phone myself, I scrolled through my two contacts. "Uh, I don't have the number."

So Kath recited what she had while I quickly dialed.

"Charmel?"

"Yes."

"It's starting!"

"What is?"

Just then the music stopped, and the parlor grew somber.

"Dad's *funeral*," I whispered hoarsely, scrunching down in my seat as the director approached the podium.

"What??" The horrified person on the other end was clearly *not* my sister!

As the formalities began, I flung a flailing look at Laura. Luckily Char's childhood bestie knew just how to reach her, finding out she was on her way.

I was mortified, but Jake was in full-out chuckle mode. We could just picture the crinkles around Dad's green eyes deepening as he grinned down mischievously too.

Act II: Starlets of the Silent Screen
Yalesville Funeral Home
Wallingford 2007

Paparazzi ambushed Grandmom's wake. No, Caroline Mae wasn't a celebrity, except maybe at the Senior Center where she generously doted on friends in need, or at home feeding neighborhood cats. By paparazzi, I mean me, or more precisely, the mamarazzi.

Gram was resting, cremated, in a tiny velvet box on a pedestal. Three weeks shy of eighty-eight candles, she probably found just as many four-leaf clovers in her life. She had that knack. But Grandmom wasn't what I zoomed in on.

My bulb was flashing for her great-grands, who looked so nice all dressed up! It was rare to have them in the same room these days, most of them outgrowing birthday parties, ranging in age from sixteen to six: Ian, Kiley, Alexandra, Michael, Maizie, and Cassie, each of us living an hour away.

I shoved the clunky camera in my purse with the idea of parlor portraits but wasn't sure I had the moxie. Was it proper etiquette? Maybe it was rude and insensitive. Would we get in trouble with the guy overseeing the event and more importantly, would the kids even cooperate?

Just as I took the plunge, I realized my son, the oldest, had already headed home with Bob. Well, Ian would've been the toughest customer to cajole anyway.

"Hey, can you all come over here for a picture?" I asked, rounding up the rest before we all split for the night. I managed to snap a few group shots in an elegant room away from the viewing.

And then taking advantage of Mom and

Joey visiting from Florida with Jake and I all in the same room, we sat for portraits too, right there in and around the stylish mauve chair as Aunt Linda clicked away.

"This is a first," the funeral coordinator quipped to Mom's husband, who could only shake his head at our nutty family. But hey, Gram wouldn't have been surprised one bit. I bet she was muttering, "Oh boy."

As the family shutterbug, everyone knew when I was around there was a camera in someone's face. But this locale was a first for me too. Gram didn't like the fuss when I pointed the lens her way, and she was probably glad, for once, she was safely out of range.

Act III: On with the Show
Center Church on the Green
New Haven 2009

My tiny mother was sixty-five and almost

"cancer-free for three" years when the throat and neck malignancies struck back with a vengeance. Cremated, half her ashes arrived up north while the rest stayed in the south. Just like in real life. Cissy, or Mommy Moo as we kids lovingly called her, split her time with family here in the summer and resided in Florida the rest of the year with her (third) husband, Doug.

We were fortunate to find just enough room in the internment area beside Gram and Aunt Bobbie, who shared a spot. My brothers and I pitched in for a stone marker and had the brilliant idea to have a Chicago Cubs emblem engraved.

When her remains arrived a few weeks later, we held a memorial service at the church. Not a fan of public speaking, Aunt Linda was gutsy and spoke anyway. I almost lost it when she ended with Mom's iconic phrase, "Sleep tight. Don't let the bedbugs bite."

I felt the need to honor Mom too,

instigator of the secret sundae society. I jotted down anecdotes on the ride over but now wasn't sure I could go through with it. With a flurry of whispered pleas back and forth, I tried passing my notes off on Bob, a presentations pro, but he refused. Which was for the best since it wouldn't mean the same coming from him. So I got up and braved the podium as well, getting in a few chuckles between the serious moments.

"I always pestered Mom to help me study. The state capitals were our favorite. And she got a kick out of my Latin flashcards. We'd fall over laughing at the forms of hic, haec, hoc, sounding like we were coughing up hairballs."

I couldn't resist wrapping up the eulogy with, "Mom taught Maizie to crochet, so don't worry, the blankets will keep on coming."

Sighing relief, but not for long, I sat down for a solemn time of prayer. Someone was supposed to sing, "Precious Lord, Take My Hand." I was shaky with dread. Even though it's a beautiful song, I heard it performed at Aunt Bobbie's funeral, and it held power to unleash floodgates I didn't want open in public. But, could it be? The soloist was a no show! So Pastor Sandra moved right along.

Wait—it seemed only right that we should sing *something*, but what? Thinking fast, I flipped through the pages of my mind. Did Mom have a favorite hymn?

Suddenly my phone blasted, "Play that Funky Music." I scrambled to shush it. Odd, I thought I had it on silent. Who could be calling when we were all here? My brothers and cousins Erick, Adam, Stacie, and Jeff grinned in amusement. Another funeral foiled by cell service. Good thing we're a casual bunch.

During fellowship in the sanctuary, a hawk appeared, flapping at a stained glass window. It looked out of place in the middle of downtown New Haven! I had the feeling it was Mom, although she always hated flying.

Did she have a bird's eye view, watching us all along? Was she shooting me "the look" or laughing at the song choice, telling us to dance silly instead, like we did in the basement way back when.

Act IV: Headliners and Curtain Calls
Back at Keenan's
West Haven 2013

When Aunt Charlotte (Dad's sister) passed from brain cancer, Aunt Linda (Mom's sister) accompanied me and Maizie to the wake. After all, our families had a long history, and she knew that side of the family better than I did.

On the way, a library came into view, and Aunt Lin suddenly veered in to renew her card.

"Now?" I asked.

"I never make it out this way," she offered. "I'm always going in the opposite direction."

Okay. It made sense, especially since wakes run in wide windows. We didn't have to be there at a specific time, and it wasn't like we had to stay for the duration.

When we made it to the vigil, we expressed sympathy to my four dapper cousins down reception row, Freddie, Robbie, Lenny, and Mike. Charlotte's boys sure knew how to look sharp and were polite gentlemen. It was such a contrast from their rowdy childhood. I explained who's who to my teenager while looking around for Jake.

"Hi. Did you have to work late?" I asked when he finally arrived. Our aunt pecked his cheek.

"No, I stopped to get a haircut." Even though it was logical, it made me laugh.

I wondered how many other people had quirky detours along the way. I was tempted to ask, thinking it would make a great book.

As usual, something always happens at these somber shindigs, and this one didn't disappoint.

After mingling, we left the building to get Chinese food. We discovered, to our horror, Aunt Linda's white passenger side door scratched with red paint!

Scanning the parking lot, there wasn't a crimson car in sight. We ended up closing the wake after all, waiting for the police while she made phone calls.

When we finally left to grab some grub, we pulled into Chip's diner. Sick with dread, Aunt Lin didn't have much appetite. I felt bad. She had gone with us mostly as a favor and this had to happen. May and I were sleeping over so we could attend the morning service, but Aunt Linda would be going to work.

Over a plate of flapjacks, I was slapped with a fabulous idea. "Maizie and I could be funeral detectives tomorrow!"

"Yeah!" Maizie agreed. "I can take photos on my phone." She was glad to have something interesting to do.

"I guess. Do you think it will work?" Aunt

Lin poked at the food on her plate.

"The same car is bound to be back, right?" The odds seemed favorable.

"Probably. Good thinking!" Her tone seemed to perk a little.

The next morning, we purposely arrived early to scout around. May had her phone camera ready. As guests arrived to pay respects, we casually strolled, sleuthing. Then, we saw it. A red car sporting white scrapes! Maizie snapped proof and included the license plate. I texted the evidence to Aunt Linda, excited to solve it.

We sat with Jake, showing him the picture. After the service, we circulated outside. We caught a glimpse of the perpetrator sliding behind the wheel. Oh, no...

Now, since I never wish to embarrass anyone, I am sworn to secrecy. Even cloaked in anonymity, it's possible certain sides of the family could figure it out. It's a frustrating scruple for a writer. It's nothing sensational, just an ironic twist of events. But if curiosity gets the better of you and you'd like to know the ending of this whodunit, you can email me at cpsmithbooks22@gmail.com, and I'd be happy to indulge. Anonymously, of course.

|19| Spinning Wheels

Shortly after his passing, my sister pushed pinwheels into the dirt around Dad's grave, lucky unplanned turf next to his mother. Cherished since childhood, these little toys were something he'd always bring her. The novelties provided more than just nostalgia. The metallic twists festively festooned the place as Pop waited for a marker.

Sis missed him so much, she took solace in their little sit-ins. Shaded by the nearby oak next to Grandma Anne's plot, she often stopped by to pour her heart out to him.

On some occasions, the spirals swirled in response. Charmel would glance around, but there was never any wind, not even a light breeze. She felt especially comforted on those days.

We didn't just leave Dad an unmarked man. Due to financial restraints all around, an official marker was delayed, but his grave was adorned in various stages.

Besides Charmel's pinwheels, I painted a tile, and it served as a temporary plaque. It was so short-lived, it cracked under pressure the first winter.

Jake put in a solar light and Ian strung an old Yankee necklace around it. We mused about tucking in Dad's favorite orange marshmallow Circus Peanuts, but we didn't want to attract ants.

Next, Cousin Freddie stepped up with an engraved garden heart. The stone served well for over a decade but began crumbling.

Long overdue, just in time for Easter 2016, we siblings chipped in for a flat marble memorial. Using the same stone smith as Mom's, we decided an acoustic guitar struck the perfect chord.

|20| Heaven Sent

Twelve miscarriages and three healthy births. That's my friend Dawn's life equation.

We met just two springs ago in Anatomy & Physiology I. Sitting behind me in the second row, she was just someone I passed papers to, but before long, she joined our little think tank. Formed in Life Science the previous semester, I was fortunate to meet a good group of gals my age. Most were going into nursing. Jen, Cindy, Dawn and I stuck together through all four sciences. She was a comrade in the crazy five-week summer edition of A&P II and in the fall, one-third of the comedy lab trio in microbiology with Cindy and me.

So when she told us the story of her fertility journey, we were practically in tears.

"The hardest loss was at 24 weeks," she

recalled, organizing her tri-color veggie chips into rows. "Even the midwife cried when I had to deliver my little girl."

"That must have been devastating," we both said to some degree. Our hearts were breaking as she continued.

"One day Child Services brought a two-year-old to my house. She screamed all the way over but stopped as soon as she walked in and little Liam offered his stuffed shark," Dawn explained. "She's a teenager now, and it's funny how much she looks like me."

"It's uncanny," we agreed.

"Yeah, I've always had this feeling my lost girl came back."

"Funny how that happens," I said.

"Yeah, especially since Nikki's birth name is actually Heaven. We kept it as her middle."

|21| Just in Time

Another outing for the "usual suspects," and that always spelled fun. It's my nickname for the common denominators involved in our capers.

All are welcome, but typically, it's the same five of us. The main three being Aunt Linda (ring leader), myself (vice ring leader), and Stacie, my cousin who's more like a sister. We were up for anything. Maizie normally fills in number four, but it was a school day. Ditto for Stacie's daughter Cassie, who used to round out the roster. These days as a busy teen, she's hard to pin down.

Sometimes if we're lucky, there's a big bunch of us, like our Christmas Cemetery gathering, followed by IHOP warm-ups nearby. Our biggest record was fourteen of us— in 2014! (I like when things match.)

This April day in 2017, something besides seafood was on the menu. More elusive than Jake, our cousin Adam was appearing! Stacie and I hadn't seen him in probably eight years.

Settling into the driver's seat for the long ride to the Connecticut shoreline, typing my aunt's address into the GPS gave me pause. What was her house number again? It was almost an anagram similar to her landline prefix, and I always had to stop and think when I addressed card envelopes. I punched in two of the three digits, but the available offerings didn't sound right.

On the next try, the anticipated choices still didn't ring a bell. I needed to hit the road, or I was going to be late. Maybe I put it in my phone contacts. I grabbed my cell to see, but I didn't need to look any further. The time of day was her exact address!

|22| Worry Knot

I come from a long line of "worriors." Grandmom, Mom and Dad, it's embedded in my DNA. Having lunch with Dawn recently, I discovered she too is a descendant.

We both *want* to be carefree, but if we anticipate every possible outcome in a situation, it's almost like good luck. Otherwise, whenever we relax and let our guard down, Meowzers, something happens.

Of course, sometimes that "something" we're expecting turns out to be nothing. Last fall, I was tormented by too many "what-ifs."

After a week in the dental hygiene program, I realized it just wasn't me anymore. Maybe if I stayed in the field.

I had an inkling it might be an old goal, but I pushed it aside, plodding along with my pre-reqs anyway. When our assignment to interview a hygienist excited me more than being one, I knew for sure.

It was a mixed bag of shaky confidence, among other things, especially the strict attendance policy. Missing clinicals meant having to pay for extra lab time. I never skip class, but you never know if you or a kid will get sick.

And then Bob announced plans for a hip replacement! How would I find time to be his caregiver? Normally I'd ride out the semester, but the program was expensive, so I grabbed the parachute and bailed during refund week.

So now what? Did I just make the biggest mistake of my life?

Perhaps the biggest problem was loose ends. I had just wrapped up all the plots in my novel when dental classes began. I still needed to edit and layer on more details. Flipping gears was tough.

But what to do about that degree? I've admired and been inspired by my mother-in-law, Mim, a retired Hospice nurse who earned a Master's in Creative Writing— in her sixties! I didn't find out about this remarkable nugget though until her memorial service in 2014 at age eighty-three. Ever since then, I began fantasizing about a writing degree someday myself.

Maybe someday was now. The closest they had was Communications. Funny, that was my major at nineteen when I started college in the first place. For once, writing was winning over practicality. And a brand new degree popped up recently—professional writing— so of course I jumped in.

Since the semester was under way, I decided to wait for the next term instead of taking an abbreviated class. Now my plate was clear for my husband's recovery. It also gave me time to polish up the novel.

Meanwhile, in the back of my mind, I still fretted about Bob's surgery. I wasn't afraid of losing him. I knew he was in the best hands God could find. After all, He orchestrated the whole works.

It was amazing really. Suddenly Bob's local orthopedist was out on medical leave. That led to reflecting on his previous doc. He was one of the best, replacing his left hip fifteen years ago in Connecticut. He really liked his manner, too.

"It's only a two-hour drive to Norwich," I said. "Try to see if you can get in. It'll be worth the trip!"

So my research scientist did some digging. There were several surgeons with the same name. And the one he was looking for no longer worked with the Norwich group. But where the awesome doctor turned up was even more astonishing—Head of Orthopedics in Worcester— closer yet!

Still, even with this perfect plan, an uneasiness festered. Bob booked medical leave between the holiday seasons. That was six long weeks of having him home. This should be a blessing, couple togetherness and all, but my hubby isn't always the cheeriest of chaps— add pain, limitations and physical therapy, and I'd have an ogre on my hands!

Funny how all the dread and heart palpations were for nothing. The newfangled surgery went smooth and fast. All went well without general anesthesia, so he bounced back quicker. He was in good spirits, hospitalized only two days. We had mini ginger ale dates.

Once home, he only needed my assistance sparingly the first day, and then magically became a one-crutch man, losing them altogether by day three. Home nurses were flabbergasted, dismissing him from care after just two visits, and he graduated from PT just as fast. He was Grandpa Joe from Willy Wonka!

Convalescence was surprisingly pleasant. Bob had pre-ordered a bunch of DVDs, and we enjoyed movie afternoons. We talked more. He worked from home, fielding emails right away. Soon he was cleared post-op and could drive again. He was back at the office two weeks early, easing in the week before

Christmas.

It was a relief to be back to normal. But how fruitless is worrying? It's absurd when we think about it. Why do we risk our health and minds stewing over circumstances that may never happen? It's a hard habit to break but like Max Lucado says, "No one can pray and worry at the same time."

|23| Pitch a Peace Tent

Anticipating a rough patch? Surround
yourself in serenity...

So you cleaned house by kicking the devil to
the curb, but a difficult person still ruffles
your feathers? Turn your house into a
spiritual retreat!

I stumbled upon this idea last summer
when I predicted a trying task ahead. I knew
the probability was high that I would hear
from a difficult person, this unstable electron
hovering on the outer ring of my nucleus. I'm
sure we all know someone like that. I wasn't
exactly looking forward to the encounter.

Fortunately, it's a rare occurrence, but
when it springs out of the blue, it unnerves
me for days. It's a complicated scenario or
else I'd cut ties completely. It sure would
make life easier. But since I can't just yet, I

could ask God for a force field. And so I began strengthening my fort. Think of it as "virtual nesting."

The first line of defense—pray for them! Even if it doesn't change the problematic party, it will transform *you*. It'll upload patience and empathy so you can look beyond the rough edges. It may seem unfair to justify their actions, but remember, you are the one reaping the reward.

Next, pad your place with positive thoughts. Push drama away. Seek laughter. Dance. Play soothing tunes.

I usually listen to an array of favorite genres from mixed decades, but during this time I let only contemporary Christian music blast from my laptop and car radio. (That's how I discovered my new favorite band, *Sidewalk Prophets*!) If metal is your speed, go for it! Or maybe you prefer classical music, gospel or traditional hymns. New-age instrumental? There's a reason why there's an "ah" in spa. Oh hey, you might as well book some "me time" while you're at it. Any reason is a good reason to pamper yourself. It's great for the mind *and* body.

Speaking of which, clear your head with a walk. On the same beat, it's good for the heart. Or break a sweat by going for a run, swim a few strokes, pedal a bike, stride a treadmill, climb a stepper. Do whatever you can to reinforce the warriors. Enlist endorphins. You know that good feeling after a workout? Those little buggers really pack a punch! They're nature's Valium, and God gave them to us for a reason. And they're free.

Get plenty of Z's, pop a daily vitamin, eat your fruit and veggies, and drink plenty of water. For a thirst-quenching resort treat, add a couple of cucumber slices!

The purpose of this preparation is to turbo-boost your happy place. Then when life hits a snag, any jabs it takes won't deplete your reserves.

Now that my tranquility troops were in order, right on cue, I heard from the dreaded person. Writing out responses ahead of time kept me on course. And since my Zen level was set to max, I managed better than before.

If people try to hook you into their drama, I've found the Polish proverb, *"Not my circus, not my monkeys,"* works wonders! Plus it's hilarious.

Whew, now that I survived *that*, I could enjoy the upcoming college road trip with Maizie and her best friend since third grade, Jill. And to top it off, we were meeting Micki and the boys, who I hadn't seen in years!

The day before our trip, I took my phone off the charger in the dining room like I did every morning. I was surprised by a text.

"Mom, I need you."

Usually, these are words empty-nesters love to hear. But he was heartbroken over a break-up. I wanted a magic wand to make it all better.

In a flurry of texts, phone calls and a lot of convincing, Ian joined us. I could better support him if we were all together, without getting tangled in the taffy-pull of worrying.

We enjoyed lunch and the artsy campus, and later, walking around Old Port with Micki proved our friendship never skipped a beat. Noah and Joseph, nearly teens, were a joy as the seven of us squeezed into quaint Captain Sam's for ice cream.

And what serendipity snapping photos with my grown kids in front of a lighthouse, spending a mini vacation together, "three peas in a pod" again, plus some! I think the change of scenery really helped Ian, at least for the first half of the weekend.

But on the second day, as we stopped at Old Orchard Beach to stroll, play putt-putt and dive hungrily into poutine, he was down in the dumps again. When we got home, he was eager to split to his.

Soaking in the pool later, I realized how drained I was. But it could have been much worse. It's a good thing I had been accruing all those extra peace points! It was just a different kind of combat than I expected.

|24| When You Wish Upon a...

Just an ordinary Saturday, scrolling through Facebook, sipping coffee like usual. Besides friends and family, I follow uplifting pieces, like local businesses, anything with dogs, recipes, April the giraffe, Donny Osmond— yes, still, especially after the spontaneously fabulous once-in-a-lifetime hug last March!

I also enjoy some light spiritual sites too. One post, "Turning to the Bible When Sorrow Strikes," from the United Methodist Church page was particularly interesting. What a great reminder Jesus understood suffering. After all, He experienced it with both hands! The idea of being able to look up comforting scriptures had me pining for my old Burgundy bound from high school confirmation days.

I lost it three moves back in 2004, a

wonder it lasted that long. Well, I thought, a Bible would be nice to have again. It sure would come in handy, especially for any scripture references for this book, even though I pop open a tab and research the internet while I'm writing anyway.

I tried visualizing a Christian book store in our area but couldn't think of any. Oh well, I'll just order one online later. It was time to run errands, so off I went with May to the supermarket.

Home again on our way up the driveway, I checked the mailbox. Among the contents was a bubble-wrapped envelope from Maizie's grandmother.

I handed the pile to her as I drove up to the house. "Don't be disappointed if it's religious," I forewarned. My sweet ex-mother-in-law, Carole, was known for her faith. I figured it was probably a cute teen-speak book on how-to-survive life after high school. Something I would have devoured at her age.

"It feels like a journal," she guessed.

After we huffed and puffed bringing in groceries then put them away, Maizie opened her package. It was a graduation bible in pretty plum!

Grandma inscribed a meaningful message to her granddaughter, still a semi-doubter with no interest in cracking it open. She might come around someday since she likes *some* of the music. In the meantime, even though it's not meant for me, I can't help but marvel at the timing.

|25| Condensation Hearts

I delight in finding random hearts. Maybe it's the hopeful romantic in me, but they sure do brighten my day. It's fun to stumble upon these comforting signs, letting us know we are in someone's thoughts. I feel reassured, as if it's telling me everything will be alright.

Last Thanksgiving, Maizie found a loving spud in a bag of potatoes. A jagged void in the snowy driveway curved into a compassionate cut-out. During my first nervous week of school, a sports bottle crinkle cheered me on. Recently out for dinner, I was surprised with a sappily shaped steak.

Two years ago, the most mystifying of all materialized on the microwave— kissed by the steam of spaghetti scrolling from the stove.

"Oh, wow! Look. Maizie, did you draw this?"

"No."

"Are you sure? You didn't doodle it a while back?" I enticed my artist with a good-natured laugh to see if she played along. If it was anyone, it had to be her.

"No," she marveled. "I don't know where it came from." I studied her face to make sure.

"You aren't pranking me, are you?" Hmm, still no wise-guy grin. My cousin was staying over. "Stacie, did you?"

"Nope. Sorry, Cuz."

"Maizie, your friends, maybe?"

I couldn't let go of logic. There was a sleepover birthday party a few weeks earlier. Surely one of the girls swirled a sweet greeting. But then again, I hadn't cooked anything to fog up a drawing surface. Still, she denied, denied, denied.

The heart had never popped up before. Could it really emerge from nowhere? I hoped so, but odd how it chose now. Tomorrow was dad's passing anniversary. Maybe the sentiment wasn't so random after all.

|26| The Pitbull Rescue

It was love at first sight.

"Joey's in the hospital. When Jim found him, he was almost dead!"

Feeling the need to sit, I fell back into a nearby swing. I was on the school playground that April day in 2010, letting Maizie and our Girl Scout troop burn off energy before we settled down on badge work or crafts.

"What? How? What was going on?"

I placed a quick call to see if my brother received the package of DVDs he left behind at our place. Grim news from his stepmother was the last thing I expected.

His dad happened to stroll by Joe's room that morning. My brother's PlayStation was blasting at nine a.m. Strange, he thought. Especially since his son was a night owl gamer and daytime snoozer.

Thanks be to God for signaling through a console! Jimmy wouldn't have barged in otherwise and found Joey barely alive. If he hadn't... I shuddered at the thought.

An ambulance whisked him away. It still isn't clear what happened, but he suffered a heart episode of some sort. Not sure if it was an actual heart attack but the best I could gather it sounded like an off kilter of electrolytes.

Backtracking a bit, you'll recall from the "Funeral Follies" Joey attending Gram's services in 2007. She passed away on his birthday, no less. He didn't know her very well but drove up to reconnect with the family. It was so nice having him lodge with us for a few days. Nobody had seen him in five years, not even Mom much, so it was great catching up. He and Buster, two redheads, hit it off immediately.

After the funeral, Mom came back with us. Grieving or not, I couldn't let Joey's birthday go by uncelebrated, so I whipped up a belated cake, complete with a Barbie candle, our running joke. We watched Pixar's "Ratatouille" that night. Mom always said Linguine, the chef in training, reminded her of Joey, so it was a special treat seeing it together.

A few days later, Joe headed out on the first leg of his long drive home. Only he didn't get very far. On a whim, he decided to stick around so, bearing coffee and doughnuts, returned to crash with our cousins Stacie, Jazzy, and Stacie's seven-year-old Cassie.

He spent the next two years chef hopping and splitting time between cousins, even road tripping twice with us during Mom's illness and end days. Eventually, he found himself back at our place before returning to his dad in Florida.

Now it was almost a year to the day of Mom's death and I had nearly lost him too! Knowing he took her departure hard, I was a little nervous, hoping this wasn't on purpose. But no, it was just a medical fluke, probably a catalyst of poor nutrition, cigarettes, and beer.

I had no idea what my little brother was going through until he spilled his heart out for this book.

After the cardiac incident, things seemed fine as he regained his health. He found work as a chef again, and that kept him busy— until two suicide attempts later. This time for real.

Only he wasn't trying to kill himself; he was trying to dissipate the cloud of despair. It was a cry for help. He was given meds and was cooking up a storm at another job, but it was still a daily struggle to get out of bed and find zest in life. He mentioned PTSD.

Which finally made sense. In 1997, he made a solid career choice joining the Navy. We cheered him on at his boot camp graduation in Great Lakes.

After further training, he beamed aboard the U.S.S. Enterprise in '98 as an airman. Eagle Scouting earned him higher pay. (He earned high wings at age thirteen!)

He was fueling planes when the

explosion hit. He wasn't injured, not physically anyway. But he was pretty freaked for the rest of his term. He kept going UA (unauthorized absence), trying to escape whenever possible. He tried self-medicating with booze, getting smashed from port to port— anything to numb the fright. He missed the boat in France, kept getting into heaps of trouble, and finally discharge papers were thrown his way. Once safe and sound back home, he discovered the love of his life had severed ties.

No wonder my usually-hilarious brother was drowning in depression and anxiety. Despite buddies, he was lonely, too.

Then in June of 2011, the pitter-patter of paws changed everything! A server had a mama pit bull that had just given birth. This perked his spirit a bit.

"Dana, save me one with a personality like mine," he suggested. So she did, giving him a considerable discount.

Joey immediately bonded with his little

beige bundle. He named her Maggie, after his favorite Chicago White Sox player, Maglio Ordonez. She even has one foot that looks like she's sporting a white sock to match.

Over time, the duo moved out on their own. They currently share a house with roommates, but Maggie still gets "grandpa" time whenever daddy's busy at the restaurant.

She's six now and a muscular seventy pounds. She's not fond of cats or squirrels— Joey's shoulder can attest to that! But she sure loves people, especially kids. And if you're lucky enough to cross paths, BEWARE. She's quite the kissy monster.

Before they met, my brother was in the pits, but falling in love with one gave him a new "leash" on life.

|27|Constellation Consolation

The stars were so vibrant; I wanted to touch them. Trudging through the woods out in the country, they brightened my path, but these were no ordinary luminaries. Their dots connected into brilliant yuletide ornaments.

Accompanying me on this journey were my parents, one on each side. We were carrying armloads of bags, trekking toward a log cabin where Grandmom was waiting to welcome us. I imagine other relatives were there too, even if they didn't make their presence known. It was going to be an old-fashioned country Christmas.

The dream was so vivid and happy, I woke up in a good mood. It was great feeling the love from my folks, which was just what I needed with the post-surgical blues.

The vision was a nice gift, but it baffled

me. First, it was early October in 2013. Secondly, even though I love woodsy settings, my family never sojourned into the sticks, never mind clinking eggnog and unwrapping gifts sans electricity.

But wait—mom and her sisters *did* grow up in a cold Pennsylvania farmhouse, sleeping under a patchwork of quilts. They even had to bundle up to use the outhouse. In the 80s, we did have Christmas gatherings in Guilford at Aunt Linda's surrounded by woods. Maybe the idea wasn't so far off, or... maybe cabin fever was setting in.

I had been camping on the couch for the past three days recuperating from knee surgery for a tibial fracture, thanks to my dog's rambunctious nature. The day before, I was feeling down. My favorite sitcoms only frustrated me more. Instead of laughing, I saw people who could get up and walk. If only I just stood still and hadn't tried to anticipate Penny's mad dash. She was finessed with her galloping figure eights. I had been replaying the mishap in my head over and over as if I could prevent the accident.

Bored, I was glad Cousin Fred was posting YouTube recordings of my dad's songs. I hadn't heard them in a long time and didn't know they existed in that media form. How remarkable mashing nostalgia with modern technology. But it had me missing Dad even more, which led to missing Mom. This spilled over into tears, of course. Was weepiness just an emotional side effect of general anesthesia?

Was the brilliant image a result of medication too? My veins slurped up a ton of the stuff in the hospital. And what was up with being heavily laden? Were they gifts for the pity party or was something telling me I was bogged down with worry for the physical task ahead? Maybe there was a greater conjurer at work, soothing my soul with the people He knew I needed the most.

|28| "Patience Cooks a Stone"

Are you anxiously awaiting something? Take comfort and a deep breath from this African proverb.

Most of the awestruck moments in this book have been small scale USA. I guess you have to go to a larger continent to find the Big Stuff, and that's exactly what happens every time my buddy Rob, his wife Lisa, and son Owen set foot on Kenya.

It makes sense when you think about it. Some of the Bible's most unfeasible feats happened right there. Well, in Egypt, anyway—baby Moses in the basket, Pharaohs, plagues, commandment tablets, burning bushes and parting Red Seas, just off the top of my head.

My friends got involved when their West

Virginia Reverend began taking missions to Nakuru, Kenya in 2011. Rob first tested the waters in 2012 by catching up with Pastor Ric and his wife Melissa who were giving seminars to local clergy, teaching them how to spread the word of God within their resources. Over the years this has led to far-flung friendships, school sponsorship, and new outlooks on life, not to mention some humorous baboon stories. (Beware, they're clever pickpockets!)

Rob's first marvel occurred at the end of his ten-day pilgrimage. Bishop Madadi invited them over for dinner before dropping them off at the airport. Meal time is very leisurely in their culture, and they don't feel rushed by the clock. So even though the Americans were enjoying the fellowship, their eight p.m. check-in window loomed near.

Nairobi is three hours from Nakuru, and

they really needed to get a move on. Finally, not wanting to be rude but pressed by the minute, they nudged everyone into the van at 4:45 pm to get the journey started. It was a smooth trip, albeit a little slow on a two-lane dirt road, but as they neared the city, dread knotted their stomachs as they became entangled in the biggest six-lane traffic tie-up Rob had ever seen—three lanes in each direction, everyone trying to wind their way around five traffic circles.

Because Nairobi was a major shipping hub and the main road to Uganda, tractor-trailers were squeezing in as well.

"You couldn't cram any more cars in this if you tried," Rob relayed, painting a painfully claustrophobic picture.

The Bishop assured him it was only a short ride once they reached the city but by the looks of the jam-packed highway, there was no way they'd make it.

Rob and the pastor's wife immediately started praying. Ric and Melissa's flight was an hour before Rob's, so it was more harried for them at the moment.

Time was ticking away, but traffic barely made progress, inching along and then at a standstill every twenty minutes, making everything more nerve-wracking than need be. If they missed their plane, no one had the means to buy extra tickets for another.

In the midst of everyone sweating bullets, Rob had an epiphany. He always knew the Lord would get them safely to Africa if that's where they were supposed to be. Wouldn't the same be true about getting home? It would be downright crazy for God to let them miss their connections now, especially after He called them down here to do His work in the first place. This was just a test to see if they remembered who was really in charge.

"You know what, guys?" Rob offered, calmer. "God's going to make something happen. He's going to delay the flight." He didn't know how but he felt it.

Breaking through the congestion fifteen minutes before takeoff spurred a scene out of "Home Alone." Melissa and her husband scurried through security then raced to the first check-in window, which to their amazement, was still open. They frantically waved their tickets at the agent.

"You know your plane leaves in ten minutes, right?" he asked.

"Yes, please hurry and process us," Melissa gushed.

Dashing through customs, fingerprint scans, and flying up the escalator like a gazelle outrunning a lion, they reached their gate. Out of breath, they encountered a long line snaking down the hall. Was this their plane or another flight out?

Theirs! They boarded in awe, collapsing gratefully into their seats.

Fifteen minutes later, the plane hadn't moved.

The pilot's voice projected over the intercom. "Ladies and Gentlemen, I'm sorry to inform you the flight is delayed. Half our crew is stuck in traffic."

Since Rob was in a different part of the airport, he had no idea what transpired with his friends. Not until he landed in Dulles and could call Lisa.

Little did he know their plane taxied off the runway just ten minutes ahead of his and they had been slumming it in Paris, now on their last leg home.

Things got official in 2015 when Ric created the organization Pastor Ric Ministries Africa.

Each time the PRM crew visits a different area, they have fun winging it. They chose independent topics without a pregame huddle and put their signature spin on sermons, presentations, and children's lessons. It all comes from the heart —and God— because somehow a theme melds together, smooth as gold. The serendipity amazes them every time. It also opens eyes and hearts to miracles of great magnitude.

Rob's wife and son first appeared on the scene in 2013. During an Amsterdam layover, Owen returned from the restroom with an African lady in tow.

"Are you his mother?"

Oh, no, what did he do? Lisa wondered, speculating what possible trouble her nine-year-old could get into in such a short time.

Well, turned out his only "crime" was wearing a Christian t-shirt which excited the woman immensely. She latched onto him, eager to share her testimony.

For years Matilda had prayed for a baby, wanting a child more than anything, but she could not conceive. Doctors told her there was no hope.

"Forget it," she was told, "It will never happen."

From what Lisa could gather, the woman did not have a womb!

Beaming, Matilda dug into her wallet and produced a photograph of a two-year-old boy. Even though the medical specialists told her it was impossible, God ignored their diagnosis and proved them wrong.

Doctors wanted to run a magnitude of tests, looking for concrete answers to this very baffling puzzle. But Matilda refused, shoving a Bible in their faces instead. "Here, this is your research!" she countered, her faith never wavering.

Extremely expensive surgery was Charles' only hope. Pastor Francis' eight-year-old had a serious heart condition.

As if the cost wasn't enough of a hurdle, Kenya didn't have the facilities to perform this particular procedure. He took his son to several doctors for second and third opinions, but the conclusions were all the same. No way could the family afford the operation or the trip to the other country.

His son was weak and growing sicker, but Pastor Francis refused to let this obstacle break anyone's spirit. He would rely on the Lord to make it possible.

Lisa and Rob's church started a prayer chain and many were fervently sending up heavenly requests for money showers before it was too late. After several persistent months, one of Lisa's friends emailed Charles' father. A powerful feeling told her the young boy was cured.

About two days later, the boy's color improved. He regained strength and energy.

The healing prompted another doctor's appointment, and lo and behold—the heart defect disappeared. There was much rejoicing and praising God.

A year later, on Lisa's return to Nakuru, she saw the miracle for herself— a robust Charles running joyously, playing and keeping up with the other children. Later, his father came to her motel and showed her the before and after X-rays.

Prayers had been abuzz for funds but the Great Surgeon went beyond the pocketbook and did one better.

|29| Another Three Dollars

When will I ever learn? Opportunities were right in front of my nose this week, and I blew it.

Maizie's meal account was three dollars short. A month left of her school career, and she finally figured out the lunch line! With so many choices, it had been too overwhelming these last four years and having anxiety only made things worse.

Recently sick of bringing PB & J's or N's (Nutella) from home, she was enticed by her friend's yummy pasta, and so she braved the trenches.

Hmm, she only purchased with cash on hand or lately, quarters since I cleaned out my purse. And on the convicted day claimed, she toted tasty leftovers.

Another kid probably mistyped their ID. No big deal, but was it our responsibility? I wasn't mad, just caught up in technicality, so I politely emailed the food services director and explained.

I'm not a cold person. I'm a pile of mush, actually. I'm all for sharing, especially if someone forgets their lunch. I just have a habit of promptly taking care of things before *I* forget. Plus, we were about to embark on an exciting event on campus: Evening with the Arts.

Senior artists were showcasing an entire wall of their best pieces. Maizie's been an amazing artist since age three, which is the perfect outlet for mental health. It's helped her thrive. She even won a partial scholarship to an art college based on her portfolio last year.

By the way, it was by sheer happenstance we settled in this small town a few years ago. We liked the quaintness and knew it had a decent school system. Bob works near the city, so we chose tranquility over congested living. But we had no idea the high school had such an esteemed art department. May and I didn't even want to move in the first place, but God knew right where to put us.

Okay, back to regularly scheduled programming. Firing off the email, I was in robot mode, computing logically. Having just arrived round trip from Connecticut with Jill didn't help matters either. After zipping the girls around for a busy best friends weekend, the blooper trickled down my brain like a game of Plinko. Realizing my misstep, I felt ashamed. Rather than request they erase the debt, which the nice director did, I wish loaves and fishes danced in my head instead.

One of my favorite miracles is when Jesus manages to have just enough food for the throng of followers with only five loaves of bread and two fish. (*Matthew 14: 13-21*) They even had leftovers, if I recall. Surely I could cover one kid's meal.

Generous Grandmom always sent in extras for others when mom and her sisters needed school supplies. Why didn't I think to pay it forward too?

To make amends, I tucked lunch money in Maizie's bag to keep on her account. She's bringing lunch again. She bought a snack, so the rest sits in credit. I better give her another buck to make things square. And the next time I switch on autopilot, I'll be sure to radio ahead for compassion.

|30| Super Ball

How resilient are you? Remember that childhood
taunt, "I'm rubber, you're glue..."

Sabotage. That's what it seemed like. Lately,
someone had been messing with my routine
and I didn't like it.

My favorite grocery store suddenly
upped and went. I didn't know until Maizie
and I pulled in and parked. Imagine our
surprise to see another franchise setting up
shop. Goodbye bag and scan-as-you-go. It was
a great time saver!

Within a month, our little pharmacy in
town was no more. I found out at a doctor's
appointment. Well, that was a fine how do
you do. The small independent chain
dissolved in surrounding towns too. Instead
of informing us, they sent our prescriptions to
the big guns.

Shortly after that, we got a letter saying

our general practitioner was leaving the health center. What was going on?

I guess we're not supposed to get too comfortable so God keeps shuffling the deck. The last one wasn't earth-shattering. We usually saw a nurse or a physician assistant anyway. And at least they sent out notes.

So we had to re-zig our zag. It was annoying, but it all worked out. We found a quieter version of a chain pharmacy. I accepted the grocery replacement over time, although I did hold a grudge there for awhile, shopping elsewhere. But when I returned after their remodel, I found I liked the place. We saved money and soon discovered their accruing gas points turned into gas cards! Just as we got into the groove, that store closed too.

I guess you could say I learned to adapt early. Right out of the gate in Chapter one, I had three third grades that year. All those moves made me buoyant. I'm that Bozo punching bag that pops back up when you take a swing. Sometimes it's punctured, cries, takes longer to inflate, but eventually bobs right back up again.

I didn't realize this until 2002, when the juggling act of marital separation, single mom-hood, and losing my dad fused together within weeks of each other. Statistically, I should've crumpled, never crawling out of bed again. Honestly, I could've used the break. But there's no rest for the weary with responsibilities, a toddler and a preteen. Being forced to function is therapeutic, but don't be afraid to seek actual counseling. The validation you receive is a real boost!

Even with helpful ways to cope, the struggles didn't magically go away. A parking ticket mocked me when I emerged from the courthouse, freshly divorced. All I could do was laugh.

Other incidents were more melancholy, like the many months I couldn't pay the mortgage on time. Even with child support, alimony, and a full-time job, I was only scraping by. I was sinking in home ownership. Was it really worth it? I didn't know how deeply embedded my worry was until several "stomach bugs" synced suspiciously with mortgage due-dates. Thanks to a one-time check from Catholic Charities, I was able to string through another month until my tax return could bail me out. Finally, I'd catch up!

Except an electrical problem shorted the house. Thank goodness I found a patient electrician with a payment plan. I love you, Brian's Electric!

In the opening act of this crazy circus, I lost a job before I found another, bringing to light a phenomenon called "blessings in disguise." When we can look beyond the circumstances, there's a faint glow. I was let go from a practice I didn't even like, but was hanging on to make ends meet.

I was unemployed for three months, going on interviews when I could get them. With patience running out, two mantras kept prancing through my head: *There's always a plan B,* and *it'll all work out somehow.* When I learned to relax a little and trust God, things fell into place. Not always perfectly, but doable.

A better fit came along at a more family friendly office, where I met Micki, then new patient Bob.

During the mortgage crisis, I managed to eke by long enough to sell the house. My neighbor had just become a real estate agent, and because of our lucky location near a casino, employees were snatching up housing like wildflowers. It sold in only two months! Believe me, there were days it felt much longer. It was a true miracle we didn't foreclose.

The surrender ripped me to shreds. Giving up meant going against my grain. Owning a house was supposed to be the grown-up thing to do, an investment. It seemed a step back, but every time I imagined us in an apartment, I felt lighter.

A friend not mentioned previously

chastised me about my choice, but I knew it was the right decision. Especially when the place I found was in the perfect location— a townhouse situated five-minutes from work, Maizie's childcare center, and elementary school which bussed her back and forth to daycare.

Is something weighing you down? Are you holding on just for the sake of logic or peer pressure because you think you're "supposed to"? Let go and be free.

When I remarried, my life went to the dogs. But that's a good thing! Except for all the shedding. Bob had a five year-old golden retriever rescue and I had the kids. We were like the old Reese's peanut butter cup commercials. Remember those? Buster immediately became my fur baby. Ian and Maizie loved him too. He's been gone five years but we still talk about his crazy antics like it was yesterday.

Sweet and gentle Buster, the mischievous sneak, sought revenge whenever we went out to dinner. He outsmarted us, even though we dog-proofed. I guess we were infringing on his time. His crimes over time included a box of 96 crayons, packets of dental floss, several chocolate infractions, a loaf of challah bread, and the oddest of all—prescription antacids, vial and all! We couldn't even fathom that one.

Because bachelor Bob used to go home to Minnesota for Christmas, I think Buster had boarding anxiety. So he was naughty during our first holiday together, tearing gift corners, even puncturing a tin of fancy cocoa like a can opener! Forcing us to wait til Christmas Eve night to set out even the mailed presents, relatives soon learned to mark gifts with Buster prohibiting signs, just in case.

Now Penny is almost five, and I didn't think loving another golden would be the same, or that another could have a goofy personality. Wrong! Penny loves people, but other dogs, not so much. She got expelled from doggy daycare because of her anxiety.

She's a tissue narc and pick pocket, sniffing out a Puffs Plus from afar, stuffing her snout in my jackets, and sometimes edging a peek of white out of my jeans as I'm wearing them. She loves anything paper, scarfing up receipts in a single leap.

She's different than Buster, and we love her every bit as much, but she hasn't replaced him. I realize our hearts are like a jigsaw puzzle. There's a specifically shaped piece for everyone we hold dear— like how enzymes only fit certain substances. Sometimes I give Penny an extra dose of hugs, hoping it passes to Buster in a golden retriever osmosis.

Her puppy days were off-the-charts in cuteness and insanity. I was against getting another dog so soon and vetoed starting over with a baby. But I was outnumbered. Meeting the litter of five didn't help either. The little culprits stole our hearts. Because I needed to kiss and cuddle a golden again, I was hooked. The four-week-old "purple girl" took a snooze on Maizie's lap and we were goners.

She came home with us a month later, and the days that followed weren't easy, even after puppy kindergarten and graduate school. Walks weren't very fun. She'd be fine, waddling along and then—Bam!—she'd suddenly become a pup possessed, lunging and nipping at my arms, ripping my clothes, sinking her teeth into me. We nicknamed her Stitch.

I called her behavior "snap dragons," but just learned it's known as "the zoomies." It refers to their running jags, too. We found this out recently when Maizie and I met one-year-old Charlotte, another golden in town. I was shocked when her person, Bonnie, had the same horror stories we did about this devilish decorum. I feel so much better knowing we're not alone.

After the first year, Penny started calming down. We enjoy her so much more now. We're very close, and I can't imagine my life without her. She's smart, sweet, and feisty. It gives her character. She's a perpetual lapdog and a mama's dog too, probably because I stayed home with her and we endured all the bumps getting here. Especially the zoomy run that sent me to the ER. After surgery with pins and a plate, physical therapy was most excruciating.

Bouncing back from a tibia plateau repair was so painful I almost resigned myself to limp the earth, but P.T. Tony's home visits, encouragement, and drive inspired me to grab my inner grit.

"I want to bump into you at Walmart one day and see you walking," he demanded.

He was serious, but I detected a jovial undertone. His gruff friendliness and voice reminded me of Food Network's Guy Fieri.

"You're much too young not to get your range back," he continued.

Was this true or was it because we were the same age at forty-nine?

Enduring his painful bends snapping scar tissue, and having to force my knee around the stationary bike, this Mount

Everest took everything I had. Around 130 is normal range, and for home visits, they shoot for 100 before graduating us to outpatient. My knee was at 85. It seemed hopeless.

While Tony pushed hard, I had to push harder. I thought of the Boston Marathon victims six months earlier. Some were vowing to *run* again. All I had to do was walk. I was determined to surpass 100. So I practiced my exercises, giving my all. Tony's last day measuring—101! By the time I was able to drive to physical therapy, it was easy as pie. And my total range came back at 133!

My shin and knee still get sore after long drives, backless shoes, or if Penny pulls too much on the leash, but I'm thankful to be back to normal.

Anything worth the trouble isn't easy. We have to put in the effort. We're all just muddling along, trying to survive. Life is always trying to knock us down. We're constantly dodging debris thrown our way. So take a deep breath, dust yourself off, and remember to bounce. You're stronger than you think. Whether your trials are small beans or far worse, God has your back. It will all work out somehow.

|31| **Charlie's** an **Angel**

Jake created our canine comic in the 80s.
He still doodles him for me on Christmas cards!

Dogs. They really make my day! Maizie and I love crossing paths with unexpected tail-waggers. We dote on Charlotte whenever we see her. Then there was Max, a bank beagle. A waiting room Maltese named Eloise, happily scampered about, greeting us all with kisses. We call it Bonus Dog Days. (Shh, don't tell Penny!) We always ask the pup's name. It's a good way to meet people too, if we remember to introduce ourselves.

The older I get, the more I appreciate all God's creatures. Have you ever really looked a horse in the eyes? A dog, cow, or even a tiger at the zoo? Just gorgeous! You can see their soul. As an animal enthusiast, this compilation wouldn't be complete without a tribute to the pooch who started it all. But fret not felines—Veeters, Blitzy, and Stan— there's been favorite other people's cats too!

Sure, I'm crazy about these woofers now, but that wasn't always the case. When I was a kid, I was *pet*rified.

As a fifth grader strolling to the store with Jake, I heard a jingle. I panicked, darting into the street. I nearly got hit by a car and all for nothing! There wasn't even a dog in sight. It happened again in eighth grade. On my way to the bus stop one dark morning, metallic clinking turned me on my heels and sent me flying home. I kissed the sidewalk instead, severely scraping my knee. I hobbled home, and Mom patched me up. At least I got out of P.E. for a few days.

I don't know where the fright came from. I never had a bad experience with dogs, except for the ones the phantom fear was causing. When I was four, I even liked the black lab visiting my grandparents' farm. Blackie, Grandmom called him. At age eleven, even though wary at first, my Guilford cousins' sheepdog, Brandy, became an annual summer favorite, but it was the sight of Bruno, their neighbor's Great Dane galloping down the hill that always freaked me out—especially the time I scrambled off the tire swing and my foot got stuck! Hearing my screams of terror, Aunt Linda rushed to the rescue and in the nick of time too, saving me from falling victim to his vicious kisses. Not only did she untangle me but Bruno's myth as well.

Pondering the fabled phobia, my mother figured her skittishness rubbed off, but as far as I know she never freaked out and risked her life. I suspect my demise had more to do with the fourth-grade teasing game my friends and I played with a big dog who lived behind our apartment building. One day out solo, he saw me. *Ut-oh*! I ran for my life and the chase was on, but I tripped on the gravel and peed my pants. Cringing, I prepared for the worst, but all he did was sniff me and trot home.

Well, whatever was causing all this canine panic, I needed to get over it and fast!

Then everything changed with Charlie. Not long after the bus stop spill, I came home from school to find a black and white terrier mix. The pound puppy was more scared than I was. He was so pathetic, my heart just melted. He was the first dog I deeply loved.

He barked ferociously at my Grease poster, protecting me from John Travolta in his Rydell sweater, burst in "singing" in protest to the drone of my table top organ, and once picked up a smiling Pac-Man ball just right, showing off an animated toothy-grin. He was a happy camper on Christmas mornings, making a neat pile of his opened toys. What a silly pup spitting out peas from his Mighty Dog dinners, yet he'd dig up Mom's scallions for a garden treat. It was his fur absorbing my tears when Football Fred turned me down for the ninth grade dance. (We had a hilarious disaster of a group bowling date instead.)

Chaz was the one I affectionately called "Frito Feet," and Joey dubbed Charlie Roo, (the rhyming pattern that led to Mommy Moo) who tagged along when Joey refreshed 10th grade and temporarily stayed with us in Newport News, turning a doggy thirteen and keeping watch under my newborn's crib.

I'm *furever* grateful Jesus sent Charlie. If not for our favorite mutt, I wouldn't know the mutual love dog companionship brings, or how pets could become such an intricate part of the family. I sure wouldn't be the canine fanatic I am today.

Couldn't the human race learn a thing or two from a pup's perspective? They approach the day never assuming anything, which avoids a lot of hurtful misunderstandings. And they're always ready to forgive. They could achieve world peace. After all, they say dog spelled backward is God.

|32| Ode To Obie

Jupiter-sized craters recently ripped through the hearts of family and friends. Labor Day 2017, Obie's lungs labored no more. We lost a great guy, Mom and her sisters' first cousin. His mother was Bea, my Grandmom Caroline's sister, and that made him patriarch of the remaining clan.

The loss is especially hard on my aunt Linda. Growing up in Pennsylvania, they were partners in crime, lifelong best friends. As adults, they talked every day on the phone. She zipped across the George Washington Bridge for frequent weekends. Because of the close relationship to Lin and Bobbie, he was a constant in my cousins' lives. The kids lovingly called him Obi Wan Kenobi, and he was quick to adorn silly nicknames back.

He shared the beach house rental for

several summers on the Jersey shore with the cousins, big and small. He popped into Connecticut for family weddings or summers Mom was up. Aunt Lin's deck rattled with nonstop laughter then.

Obie was infamous for hilarity. Forever the life of the party—he had King Midas' touch with a twist, making everyone feel special. It was easy to forget your woes when Obie was around.

We were lucky to friend him on Facebook the year he logged on. His witty and uplifting "Birthday Shout-Outs" always came with kind kudos. I think all his pals and the large caboodle of cousins got one in before he passed. He was such a joy. Some were just getting acquainted, and we all wish he was online sooner.

Three road trips to Florida when Mom was sick, we'd detour to Pennsylvania on the way back. Obie blessed us with dinner entertainment "Under the Pier," a tasty seafood joint, the kind with newspaper placemats and funny restroom names. Obie worked there for decades but had retired by then. Next door was the best creamiest soft serve ever!

By the last stretch, it struck me funny how we kept bringing him a different mix of us, a click of a Rubik's cube each time. **First trip**: Joey, Maizie, me and Aunt Lin. **Trip two**: Maizie, Ian, me and Aunt Lin. **Trip three**: Joey, Jake, me, and Aunt Lin. On the last trip, Jake was craving cheese steaks, so we shook things up at a *hoagie* place instead. (Another of his nicknames graced by Stacie, who got zinged with Tracy right back.)

The fall of 2016, I got the privilege of getting to know him better. He selflessly stepped up as a test reader for my spy romance when I sent out begging notices. He got a bonus for signing up: Maizie's amazing chocolate chip cookies.

I recruited him because of his grammar genius and I wasn't wrong. He gave me invaluable adverb advice.

"If I have to read another ruefully, nervously, awkwardly, I'll scream. But what do I know, I'm just a cranky old man."

Lesson learned. He made me laugh so I quickly cleaned house, chucking most. I already suspected those pesky buggers were bogging down my dialogue. I'm glad he said something. Funny, the last thing Obie seemed was cranky—or old! I'm convinced he and equally fun Aunt Linda found the fountain of youth and buried the map in a secret location.

The real treasure of having Obie as a test reader was this new interaction. I loved how my book created an excuse for more conversations between us!

He messaged me as we cheered on the Cubs in the World Series, dubbing Baez a favorite player in the bunch in this bittersweet victory knowing they were Mom's team. She would have been over the moon with their Championship win! Maybe she already was.

Just the other day, close friend Joe in California was at a stop light when a pickup truck idled beside him. He noticed a sticker on the back passenger window. "O.B." Curious initials cradled by an angel wing.

Pennsylvania friend Jenn spent a day seeing the number 203 everywhere. She couldn't figure out why until it dawned on her— it was Obie's apartment number. His P.A. cousin, Janice, recently had a birthday and Obie appeared in her dream, still doing shout-outs from beyond!

On his birthday, Aunt Linda discovered a teeny feather in her house. The same day, Jenn came out of a store and discovered a feather tucked beside the driver's side tire. Taking a pic to post on Facebook, she hopped in, scratching off a lottery ticket. She won $30 so she got out to cash in. The feather was gone, no wind or breeze.

Then Aunt Lin discovered a feather on her car's console. Jenn was behind a car with a license plate 1017—his birthday. He's one busy angel, hovering near.

|33| Parting Words

"Caroline!"

In 1970, Grandmom woke in the middle of the night to the sound of her name and a nudging on her foot. She turned to my grandfather, but he was fast asleep. Instead, she saw her father's spirit at the end of the bed. Then he vanished.

The next morning, news of his passing reached Gram.

In the same year, she lost her mother. I remember hearing how on some random night, she saw her too.

"Wasn't she afraid?" I asked my mom.

"No, she knew her mother would never hurt her."

True, but still...

Stacie accounts an incident two weeks after losing her mother, Bobbie, in 2000. She was putting eight-month-old Cassie to bed after a middle of the night waking. She left the kitchen light on and went back to snap it off.

As soon as she did, she saw her mother sitting on the couch. "Go to sleep. I'll watch over Cassie."

Stacie froze. When the image faded, she scampered to her room, deciding not to wake her husband for fear he'd think she was crazy. Falling asleep, she knew everything was going to be okay.

I've never seen a ghost, but I think I'd faint if I did. I'm thankful Dad chose to travel the telephone lines and my folks stick to dream sequences.

Still, wistfulness and a challenging Villanelle assignment inspired "Stay for Tea," as I imagined my parents and loved ones stopping by for a spot.

The theme may sound a bit macabre, but we had to whip up the beginning stanza's first and third lines from a random handful of magnetic words. From the limited options, the idea of hosting a ghostly tea party came to mind.

Every middle verse serves as an echo, rhyming with each other. (Read it all together and then for fun read just the middle lines) The first line gets flipped to the third position in the second and fourth stanzas and so on. I've labored over this several times, but I'm still not sure I've gotten the cadence right. It's a very tricky form indeed.

Stay for Tea

A haunted desire blind of breath
Departure date scribed upon the grave
From marble & wood, we celebrate death

A poof of dust, they suddenly left
Sorrow and guilt, grief's greatest slaves
A haunted desire blind of breath

Celestial beings, their talents bequest
Cascading through branches, our lineage saved
From marble & wood, we celebrate death

Frankensteinian efforts help fetch
Stitching together the words you bade
A haunted desire blind of breath

Eternal love gleams with the family crest
Honor untethered, shadows so brave
From marble & wood, we celebrate death

Cobwebs & doilies conjure my guests
Linger a spell, let me savor and crave
A haunted desire blind of breath
From marble & wood, we celebrate death

~Chele 2/9/2016

Jeanette has an interesting theory about ghosts. While she doesn't believe in scary apparitions per se, she does think God sends messages to us in a recognizable form.

For instance, her mom had a delightful drop-in and detailed discussion with her deceased dad (Nette's grandpa) in the wee hours putting Easter baskets together. Now, even though Betty may have been punchy from the late hour, Jeanette believes she did communicate with her father in some way.

Seeing isn't the only way to believe. Sometimes spirits tickle our other senses too.

Nette's paternal grandfather had voluminous blooms at his funeral. Sometime later, her grandmother remarried.

At the small ceremony, Jeanette's dad remarked, "Do you smell flowers?"

"Yes!" Nette agreed, inhaling a strong scent. They surveyed the area, but there wasn't a petal in sight. Surely Grandpa was blessing the new union!

Sometimes out of the blue, I get a whiff of Dad's Aramis cologne. Working at the supermarket pharmacy, it happened a few times. I figured a heavy-handed customer waltzed by. When it happened again, during a slow Saturday in 2011, I decided to investigate once and for all. I snooped every aisle but found no one giving off the familiar fragrance.

Fellow nonsmoker Aunt Linda reported a strong cigarette scent by her bed after her sister Bobbie passed. It still happens occasionally. When it does, she says, "Hi

Bobbie, Hi Cissy," appreciating both sisters' unexpected pop-ins.

On rare occasions, I smell cigarettes at home too. And sometimes for no reason at all, I get the feeling my mother is hovering near.

We may lose the ones we love, but they are never really far away, are they?

Beyond the Blessings

Hi, I'm Michele, or Chele for short. I cherish my readers! Without you, I'm just entertaining myself. Thank you for venturing into my world of mini-miracles. Sometimes it's the small blessings that leave the biggest impact. I love to include bonus material, so be sure to read my books to the very end.

Have a coincidence to share, questions, or want to say hello? I'd love to know.

Connect with Chele:

cpsmithbooks22@gmail.com.

Like something you've read? Please consider jotting a review on retail sites, Bookbub or Goodreads, and follow my author pages and social media for book updates.

Writing is like a time machine. Revisiting these segments really took me back. Especially the Jesus '81 Festival. I always wanted to go to another, but we moved shortly after. And I must have really had it bad for poor Geoff. I've noticed his name has subconsciously crept into other characters as well, and I'm planning to incorporate my crush antics gone wrong in another work.

The art of prose also has a Lazarus effect. Suddenly the words breathe life into my loved ones and I'm with them again. But one of my favorite aspects of this project is telling people about it. Someone always has an incredible incident to dish back. It's exciting to hear examples of unexplainable events that could only come from the Good Lord above. It makes for interesting small talk during haircuts, pedicures and awkward doctor moments. And who knows, maybe I'll collect enough juicy morsels for another book.

Fiction by Chele Pedersen Smith
Behind Frenemy Lines: a spy romance mystery
The Epochracy Files: time-twisting tales
Chronicle of the Century: time capsule mystery

Bonus material

Rejection Collection

The word "no" makes us better. How many times do
you hear it?

Rejected writer. That was the name of my first blog. Maizie set it up for me ironically and we laughed. Upon thinking about it, really dissecting what it meant, I decided to own it. It defines me. It made me the writer I am today.

I've been writing since third grade if you count my very first booklet about a comical rainy day. Inspired by Grandmom's gift of stationery supplies, I was intrigued by the handheld hole punch and strung a stack of paper together with string.

In sixth grade, my friend Debby and I won the school's hobby contest with our stapled April and Cherry "books." Besides writing, Debby had quite a drawing talent, especially horses. I think of her often and wonder where she is today.

In eighth, I began a Sherri Whitman teen mystery series I wrote past high school. Ideas formed in history class based on a few words on the board. For one, Richmond, Virginia.

Bam, I had the setting even though I had never stepped foot there—until I happened to meet Barry!

Friends would devour my Sherri booklets as soon as I set down the pen, sometimes on the bus ride home. Thankfully one gal served as a brilliant editor and corrected my grammar mistakes, like "could of" instead of "could've." Those lessons still stick with me today.

I dug out the Sherri mysteries when May was twelve and she got a kick out of them too. She wants me to publish those next, which is fitting because a more mature installment of those mysteries was my first ever submission to publishing houses when I was twenty-one. It also spurred my first series of rejections.

Scholastic was the only one to give constructive critique, even tossing in two young-adult paperbacks to read as examples. I'm grateful they took me seriously. No wonder I've always loved their school book fairs!

I can't help but think if I hadn't received constant refusals from publishers and periodicals over the last thirty years, this book wouldn't exist. I thank God for self-publishing and high school alum Mary who paved the way, showed me the ropes, and became my mentor.

In the late 80s, despite the naysayers of the magazine world, I'd churned out fictional short stories for Redbook contests and more fervently, creative nonfiction for a certain periodical. I'd snail mail the manuscripts, hold my breath, then receive the letdown via a polite form letter stapled to my story. I learned to dread those bulky self-addressed suckers.

The first in this collection was my 2000 submission "Point of Sail," then called "Smooth Sailing," followed by a 2002 primitive, long and complicated edition of chapter 10's, "The Pearly Gates Phone Company," then called "Hello from Hippie Heaven." I'd bum out, take a break and live life as a working mom. I kept my tools sharpened with family newsletters but whenever inspiration hit, I'd bang out the next spiritual short, pray, fingers crossed, and submit again. It was a continuous loop. A very slow vicious circle.

Einstein said the definition of insanity was doing the same thing over and over and expecting a different result. Well then, I must be crazy.

A few years ago my rejections bumped up to first class. I received two handwritten notes! Maybe because of better revisions. Rejection ignites the fire to improve. It fuels defiance. In 2014, an editor's scribbling followed a fresher, tighter remake of "Hippie Heaven," then called "A Call from Heaven."

"I like it," he said. "But it's more of an essay. Do you have anything different?"

Boy, did I. Having just finished writing an earlier version of "The Pancake Parable," then called "Spatula Story," I polished it up and sent it out immediately. It was quirky. It couldn't get any more different than that. I had a good feeling about this one.

Except another fat bundle arrived with a sprawled note attached, this one a bit harder to decipher. Cousin Stacie helped me figure it out.

"I like it, but I don't see the deeper meaning," the editor said this time. "I don't see how it can help readers. Still sounds more like an essay."

Hmm. Maybe dads view the empty-nest differently. His comments revved up another round of revisions. I added a fresher style and more dialogue, but what about that deeper meaning? Suddenly I was lit with the epiphany of comparing Jesus to Old Trusty. It became the glue. Now I can't even fathom the story without it. I mailed off the new version right away, but never heard a thing. I read somewhere later that writers should not send a revised piece back to an editor unless solicited. Oops, rookie mistake.

Regardless, I felt so close now I could

almost smell the ink hot off the printing press.

Still, something bothered me. What was I doing wrong? My work seemed similar to their story style. I've been an avid fan for thirty years, but the frustration of not being good enough made me mad. I chucked the latest issue across the room, tempted to cancel my subscription. I felt guilty for acting like a brat yet something kept me connected.

I took a break, enrolling in a creative writing class just for fun and focused my attention elsewhere.

Pretty soon I was at it again. I polished up "The Call from Heaven" and tightened it with a vise, giving it more life with additional dialogue. Then the perfect whimsical name came to me! An hour after submitting the solo story of "The Pearly Gates Phone Company" online to their spin-off magazine, an editor *called!* He was interested. He was going to pitch it at the next meeting. I soared. I was actually talking to an editor! My goal was coming true! He would let me know in three weeks.

Except, he did not. Emailing him, I discovered the truth. They didn't want stories dealing with death. *Really, since when all of a sudden? No fair!*

"Do you have any lighthearted miracles in 150 words or less?" he asked instead. "Something like your pinwheels and your West Heaven bank receipt, only not death related."

I reached deep into my thinking cap and wrote a blurb, whittling down as much as possible. It's very challenging, but a great writing exercise. I launched it only to get shot down. I went back to the drawing board and after each, "Sorry, it's not what I'm looking for," decided to give up. It was frustrating not being able to please these publications.

Yet, every so often, I kept carving out more. "SOS," "Eviction Notice" "God loves a Fearful/Cheerful Giver" and "Hummingbird Hangout," soon filled my document list, but I guess they didn't have the wow factor he was looking for.

I wanted to scream, "Take the Pearly Gates, it's the best one. You liked it before!" But by this time he quit answering my emails.

I was beginning to believe those memes on Facebook; you know the ones saying something like, "When you knock on a door, and it doesn't open, it's not yours."

Not long after receiving those hopeful handwritten rejections, we were visiting Bob's family in Minnesota after his mother passed away. I tried cheering up my sister-in-law. She was feeling bad for not being there the moment her mother died, even though she was about to head over and had been there all week despite a full-time job. I recited the sentence from "Pearly Gates"—how guilt is deceiving, convincing us we can never do enough. She and Bob agreed it was true. To lighten the mood, I related the two cell phone bloopers that became the "Funeral Follies," making them laugh. Then I lamented my latest publishing blows and close calls.

"I want to be a real writer, but it looks like it will never happen," I relayed over coffee.

"You don't have to be published to be a real writer," she said, to the effect of, "You write, therefore you're a writer."

She was right. It was a relief to take the edge off my goal.

Besides, I was in good company. Just about every author or artist got the nopes before making it. This includes JK Rowling, my other favorite— Judy Blume, and even the Beatles! According to litrejections.com, Beatrix Potter took matters into her own hands and self-published 250 copies of "The Tales of Peter Rabbit," and that was way before computers!

Then I saw a social media post from longtime friend Deedee about a new physiological thriller available by M.P. McDonald. She credited her best friend, Mary. Because of the same last name, I thought she was kidding, but the awesome news was true! I was happy for her, but suddenly the Green-eyed Monster woke up and kicked me in the pants. "That's supposed to be your goal, dummy!"

As high school alums, I friended Mary on Facebook and bent her ear. She told me about this crazy thing called an electronic book. I'm so *old school*, my visions of publishing went only paper deep. Now a whole new world opened up. I was antsy to try it, but my novel was only half done. I saved all the info she gave me, including tips on finding a great cover designer, too. From her sample ideas, I found Steven Novak, who wows me every time.

During semester breaks I typed away on my spy romance, heavily editing. She helped me through the steps when it was ready. When I uploaded the cover and pages of "Behind Frenemy Lines" and saw a sample launch on the preview reader for the first time, I was thrilled!

"It looks like a real book!" I gushed to

Mary.

"It *is* a real book!" she typed back, laughing.

What a feeling! Thanks to her, I started 2017 with a published dream! It's wonderfully surreal watching an ambition materialize. It's funny too. Not long before, I couldn't wrap my head around an e-book, yet here I was sort of tech savvy! Best of all, I had a George McFly moment when the paperback arrived.

Now what about a second book? Since I had those six spiritual snippets, I was racking up quite a collection, but did I have enough to publish them myself? I ran what I had through the revision ringer and then created a bunch more to round it out. When family and friends told me their stories, I wrote those too.

Since the year 2000, I've wanted to write "Planting Crayons." My vision was more of a children's book, but I'm so glad this compilation jogged my memory and made it possible.

Who knows, maybe I'll keep submitting to that magazine. It's comforting to know it's not my only venue. If my dream came true, so can yours! Whatever your goal, don't listen to downers, especially if it's the voice in your own head. Pray for guidance, pump yourself up, and take matters into your own hands. Make it happen. And if you run into rejections, look at them as reflections instead.

*Update June/July 2019: I got in! And this time I wasn't even trying. Out of the blue, I received a call from a *Guideposts* editor.

"We want to use your hummingbird story in our 'What Prayer Can Do' section this summer."

What?? Was I dreaming? Excited, blessed and extremely grateful, my head spun in awe! I sent that piece in three years ago. See, it's all in God's timing.

About the Author

Chele lives in North Central Massachusetts with her scientist guy, Bob, grownish daughter, "Maizie," and their feisty golden retriever, Penny. When she's not on the lookout for mini-miracles or penning prose, Chele is a pharmacy tech and college writing tutor, FRIENDS fanatic, and along with Maizie, loves dressing up their dogs for holiday photo ops.

Penny, the Halloween fairy, 2016

Buster's cap during a New Year's Day nap 2011

Made in the USA
Middletown, DE
29 May 2021